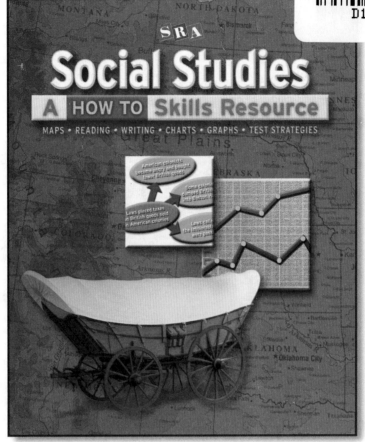

Social Studies
A HOW TO Skills Resource
MAPS • READING • WRITING • CHARTS • GRAPHS • TEST STRATEGIES

Consulting Authors

Richard G. Boehm, Professor
Director of the Grosvenor Center for
  Geographic Education, and Jesse H.
  Jones Distinguished Chair in Geographic
  Education
Southwest Texas State University
San Marcos, Texas

Brenda Webb, Assistant Professor
Kilby Laboratory School
University of North Alabama
Florence, Alabama

A Division of The McGraw-Hill Companies

Columbus, Ohio

Program Reviewers

Kathleen Boyd
Teacher
Ozaukee Elementary School
Fredonia, Wisconsin

Michelle Maresh
Teacher
Yucca Valley Elementary School
Yucca Valley, California

Linda Simonetta
Teacher
Carrie Martin Elementary School
Loveland, Colorado

Mark A. Smith
Teacher
Oquirrh Elementary School
West Jordan, Utah

Assessment Specialist

Michael Milone, Ph.D.
Placitas, New Mexico

www.sra4kids.com

SRA/McGraw-Hill

A Division of The McGraw·Hill Companies

Send all inquiries to:
SRA/McGraw-Hill
8787 Orion Place
Columbus, OH 43240-4027

Printed in the United States of America.

ISBN 0-07-569252-X

1 2 3 4 5 6 7 8 9 RRC 07 06 05 04 03 02 01

TABLE OF CONTENTS

Map Skills

Reading and Thinking Skills

Writing and Research Skills

Chart and Graph Skills

Test-Taking Strategies

Map Skills

Skill 1
HOW TO
Read a Map

Read Me Like a Book

Reading a map means understanding what all the symbols, lines, shapes, colors, and words on the map mean. Together, these features form a picture describing the location of a place in the world. Being able to read maps is an important and useful skill.

There are two basic types of maps: general purpose maps and special purpose maps. General purpose maps (or *general reference maps*) show cities, countries, or continents, as well as roads, rivers, and oceans. Examples of special purpose maps (also called *thematic maps*) are climate maps, product maps, and population maps. A map can be drawn for almost anything. There are maps that show the depths of oceans and maps that show the positions of stars in the sky.

Two kinds of general purpose maps are physical maps and political maps. A **political map** shows the boundaries that people have created, such as the border lines around a city, state, province or country.

A **physical map** shows the natural features of a place, such as mountains, lakes, deserts, and valleys. No single map can show everything about a place. Every map gives only certain information.

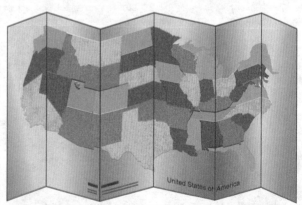

United States of America

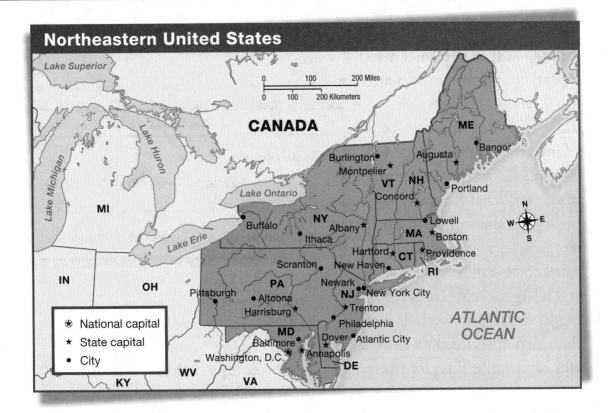

Northeastern United States

Lake Superior

0   100   200 Miles
0   100   200 Kilometers

CANADA

ME

Bangor

Burlington•
Montpelier ★   Augusta ★

VT   NH
Concord ★   •Portland

Lake Ontario

MI

Buffalo•   NY
Albany ★   •Lowell
Ithaca•   MA   ★Boston

Lake Erie

Hartford ★   •Providence
Scranton•   New Haven•   CT
RI

IN   OH   Newark★
Pittsburgh•   PA   New York City
•Altoona   NJ•
Harrisburg ★   ★Trenton

Philadelphia•

⊛ National capital
★ State capital
• City

MD   Dover•Atlantic City
Baltimore•   ★
Washington, D.C.⊛   ★Annapolis
KY   WV   VA   DE

ATLANTIC
OCEAN

N
W   E
S

The eye can zoom in on and out from a map like a camera can zoom in on or out from a scene. Look at the whole map first. Then zoom in on the following four parts that explain what is being shown.

The map **title** tells what the map is showing. The title will often tell the type of map (political, physical, or other). Sometimes, maps will show surrounding areas. For example, a map of the United States might show parts of Canada and Mexico. Reading the map title will help you know which area of the world is the focus of the map.

TIPS

➤ **The map title sometimes appears in the map legend.**

➤ **Different kinds of maps give different kinds of information. Sometimes you must use more than one map of a place to get all the information you need.**

The **legend,** or **key,** on a map tells what the symbols on the map stand for. The legend is usually found in a corner of the map. Many maps use small pictures, or symbols, to represent cities, roads, and other features. In the legend shown here, a star represents a state capital; a small circle stands for a city; and a larger circle stands for a bigger city. Other symbols include thick dark lines for state boundaries and curved blue lines for rivers.

Legend	
★ State capital	〜〜 River
● City under 500,000	—— State boundary
● City over 500,000	—— Country border
▲ National park	⋀⋁⋀⋁ Mountains

Map legend

The **compass rose** is a symbol that shows direction on a map.

Some compass roses show only the directional arrows of North, South, East, and West. Sometimes the arrows appear in a circle, just like they do on an actual compass. This compass rose shows the four main (or *cardinal*) directions as well as four intermediate directions of Northeast, Northwest, Southeast, and Southwest.

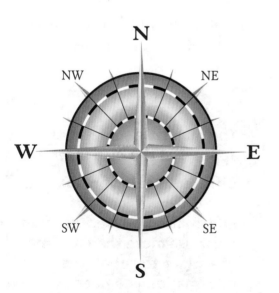

Compass rose

The **map scale** tells how to measure distance on the map. The scale is a line marked in miles, kilometers, or both. One inch or centimeter on the scale might represent 100 miles, 1,000 miles, or some other number of miles. The scale may be printed in the legend, or it may appear elsewhere on the map.

TIP Some compass roses show north with either a larger directional arrow or by itself. When you are facing north, east will always be on your right and west will always be on your left. When you know one direction, you can figure out the other directions.

A map's scale shows the relationship between distance on the map and distance in the real world. The simple scale on this page shows that one inch equals 100 miles (and that one centimeter equals 125 kilometers). How can you tell that the line is one inch long? You have to measure it with a ruler. You also can use a piece of paper to help you measure distance on a map. Draw or trace the scale onto the piece of paper. Then position the piece of paper on the map and measure how far one place is from another.

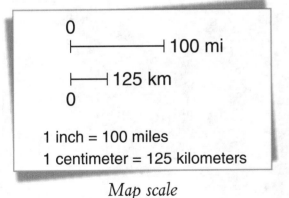

1 inch = 100 miles
1 centimeter = 125 kilometers

Map scale

Study the map of the United States below. The map features are labeled.

Different colors are used to help you tell the states apart from one another.

Title

Compass rose

Scale

Legend

The United States of America

USE THIS SKILL

Read a Map

Use the map of the United States on page 8 to answer these questions.

1. Is the map a political map or a physical map? How do you know?

2. What color is used for the state of Maine? What color is the neighboring state of New Hampshire?

3. What is the capital of New Mexico?

4. How many miles is New Mexico's capital from the nation's capital?

5. Which direction is South Dakota from Kansas?

6. In what direction would you travel to go from Austin, Texas, to the city of Los Angeles, California?

7. Which state is northeast of Kentucky?

8. How many kilometers is it from Denver, Colorado, to Salem, Oregon?

TEST TIP If a test asks questions about distance, sometimes you will have to make an estimate or guess the distance. Remember, the correct answer will be the **closest** estimate, not an exact answer.

Skill 2
HOW TO
Read a City Map

The City of Trees

There are 32 Peachtree Streets in the city of Atlanta, Georgia! Atlanta is a city where people might need a city map to find the street or place where they want to go. People use city maps to find streets, buildings, parks, museums, shops, and restaurants.

A **city map** is a map that shows the important features, or details, of a city. City maps show streets, airports, subways, important buildings, parks, and other points of interest. A city map may also show the highways leading into or out of the city.

When you study the Civil War of the nineteenth century or the civil rights movement of the twentieth century, you will read about the city of Atlanta. You might use maps. City maps can serve as a link between history and geography. After reading or hearing about an event in a city's past or present, looking at a city map might help you better visualize the event.

Read a book or a map to learn about cities.

Cities may be small or large. They have definite boundaries, important histories, and interesting landmarks. Many books have been written about cities. Books often include maps to help readers see a city's exact location and the locations of points of interest.

Just as you use your imagination when you read a book, you also use your imagination when you look at a map. If you have visited or lived in Georgia, you might look at the map below and remember the trees, smells, and sights. If you live in another part of the country, you may have ideas about the state of Georgia or about the southern United States.

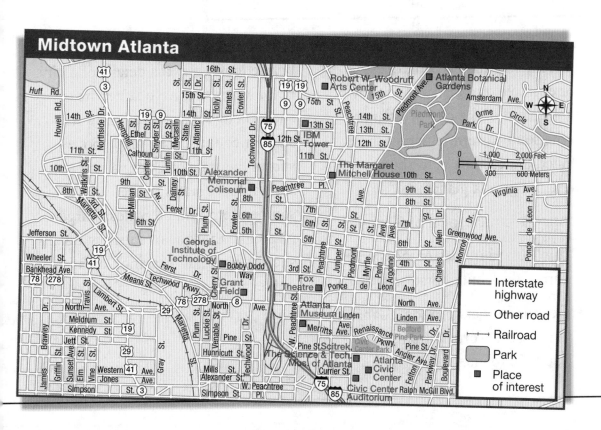

Midtown Atlanta

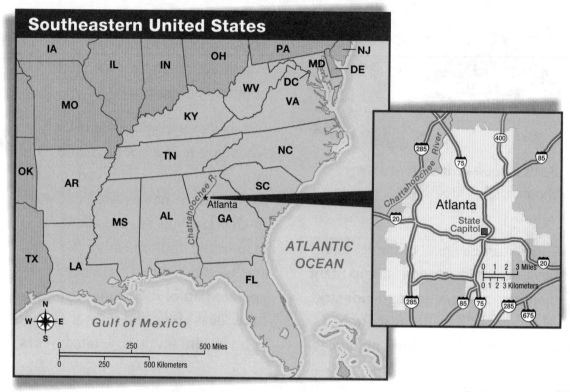

Southeastern United States

A map "describes" a place in a different way than a book does. For example, the map above shows the location of the city of Atlanta in the southeastern region of the United States. The map shows these things at a glance:

- Atlanta is the capital of Georgia.

- It is located in the southeastern part of the United States.

- Georgia borders Florida, Alabama, Tennessee, North Carolina, and South Carolina.

A state map is a helpful place to start before looking at the details of a city map. Maps that have larger areas show a city's exact location in its state or country. The map above shows the state of Georgia and several other states in the southeastern United States. Large maps like this one often show details such as national recreation areas, universities, and memorial parks.

The history of Atlanta dates back to a Cherokee village called "Standing Peachtree," which was first seen by European explorers in 1782. The village became Fort Peachtree during the War of 1812. Then, in 1837, the town of *Terminus* was established at the beginning of the Western and Atlantic Railroad. The town was renamed *Marthasville,* and then in 1845 it became *Atlanta.*

Railroads played an important role during the Civil War. They moved soldiers and supplies all over the South. In 1864, the famous Battle of Atlanta left the city in ruins. Only 400 of the city's original 4,000 buildings stand today. But the people of Atlanta have worked hard to rebuild their city. Today, the city hosts international exhibitions and attracts new residents.

TIP Sometimes, small cities grow into large cities. Atlanta was a small city that over the years blossomed into the large city that it is today.

Like all maps, city maps have several features. These features are provided to help you read city maps. The map title tells you what city is being shown. The compass rose shows direction on a map. The four main directions, or **cardinal directions,** are *North, South, East,* and *West.* The **intermediate directions** between each main direction are *Northeast, Northwest, Southeast,* and *Southwest.* The map scale tells you how distances on a city map compare to actual distances in the real city. See examples of these features using the city map of Atlanta on the next page.

Peach trees

Study the city map of Atlanta below. Notice how the map features help you read the map.

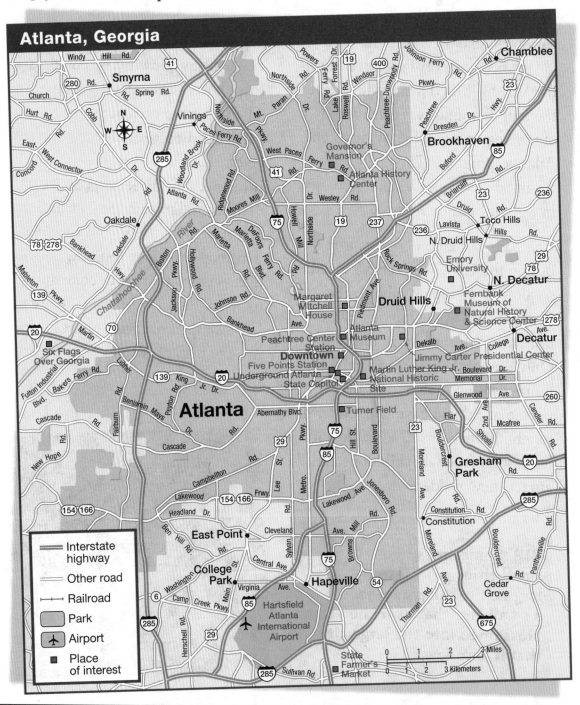

Atlanta, Georgia

Read a City Map

Use the city map of Atlanta on page 14 to answer these questions.

1. What direction is the airport from downtown Atlanta?

2. What is the name of the river that flows through the northwestern part of Atlanta?

3. Does Wesley Road run east and west or north and south?

4. How far is the Margaret Mitchell House from the Atlanta History Center?

5. In which direction does Northside Drive run?

6. Which is closer to the state capitol: the Atlanta Museum or Underground Atlanta (an area of shops and restaurants)?

7. What major highway would take you from Turner Field to the State Farmer's Market?

8. If you wanted to walk from the Martin Luther King, Jr. National Historic site to the state capitol, in which direction would you go?

9. Is Peachtree Center Station northeast or northwest of Five Points Station?

10. How far apart are Turner Field and Emory University?

TEST TIP

When a test asks questions about a city map, first skim the map to understand it. Look back at the map for details as you answer each question.

HOW TO

Read a State Map

O-Y-O

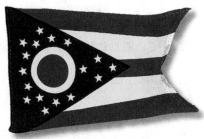

State Flag of Ohio

The state of Ohio takes its name from the Ohio River. The river forms the state's southern boundary and also part of its eastern boundary. French explorers named the river, using the Seneca-Iroquois word *oheo* ("o-why-o") for "beautiful." Ohio has thousands of miles of rivers and streams, many natural resources, and an interesting history.

Travelers can use a **state map** to find their way from one city or place in a state to another. A state map can be used to learn about the geography of a state. State maps use symbols, lines, colors, and

words to highlight historical sites, large rivers, roads, and cities. State maps are reference sources just like books, encyclopedias, and Internet sources are.

Some maps show other states bordering the state that is the subject of the map. Before looking at a state map, you may find that studying a regional map is useful. **Regional maps** show entire areas where the land or culture has common features. The map on the next page shows that Ohio is located in the Great Lakes region of the United States. States may belong to more than one region. For example, the state of Ohio is also part of the Midwest region.

Ohio's state bird, the cardinal

Native American groups such as the Chippewa, the Delaware, the Shawnee, and the Wyandot lived in the Ohio territory long before European settlers. Because of its many waterways and varied wildlife, the area that became the state of Ohio attracted people from other parts of the country. Travelers and traders from the original thirteen colonies moved into the region. In 1803, Ohio became the seventeenth state to join the union. After the Civil War, gas and oil industries were established in Ohio.

TIP When you look at a state map, find the state's borders. A state may be bordered by a lake or river, an ocean, another state, or even another country.

Columbus, once a small settlement, became the state's capital in 1816. A state's **capital** is the city where the state government is located. A capital is often marked with a star on a map. Look at the map on the next page to find Columbus, Ohio.

Great Lakes Region

When North America was first settled by Europeans, many people traveled on the Ohio River. Some made their way to the Mississippi River and then southward.

Study the map of Ohio below. The map shows how Lake Erie to the north, and the Ohio River to the east and south, form **natural boundaries** for the state. Ohio's western boundary is a straight **geometric boundary,** which is shaped by people, not by nature.

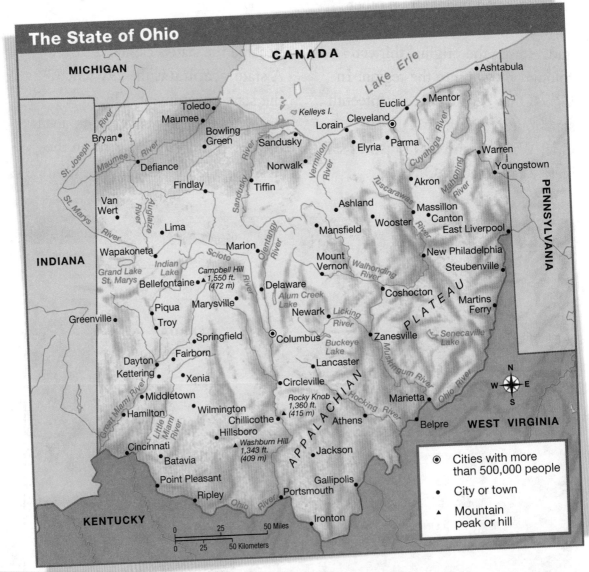

The State of Ohio

CANADA

MICHIGAN

Lake Erie

Ashtabula

Toledo
Maumee
Bowling
Green
Sandusky
Kelleys I.
Lorain
Euclid
Cleveland
Mentor
Bryan
St. Joseph River
Maumee River
Defiance
Norwalk
Elyria
Parma
Vermillion River
Cuyahoga River
Warren
Youngstown
Findlay
Tiffin
Akron
Mahoning River
St. Marys
Van
Wert
Auglaize River
Lima
Sandusky River
Ashland
Mansfield
Massillon
Wooster
Canton
East Liverpool
Tuscarawas River
Wapakoneta
Marion
Scioto River
Olentangy River
Mount
Vernon
Walhonding River
New Philadelphia
Steubenville
PENNSYLVANIA
INDIANA
Grand Lake
St. Marys
Indian
Lake
Campbell Hill
▲ 1,550 ft.
(472 m)
Bellefontaine
Delaware
Alum Creek
Lake
Coshocton
PLATEAU
Martins
Ferry
Piqua
Marysville
Newark
Licking
River
Greenville
Troy
Springfield
Columbus
Buckeye
Lake
Zanesville
Senecaville
Lake
Fairborn
Lancaster
Muskingum River
Dayton
Kettering
Xenia
Circleville
APPALACHIAN
Marietta
Ohio River
N
W E
S
Middletown
Rocky Knob
1,360 ft.
▲ (415 m)
Hocking River
Athens
Belpre
WEST VIRGINIA
Hamilton
Wilmington
Chillicothe
Hillsboro
Great Miami River
Little Miami River
Cincinnati
Washburn Hill
▲ 1,343 ft.
(409 m)
Jackson
Batavia
Point Pleasant
Gallipolis
Portsmouth
Ripley
Ohio River
KENTUCKY
Ironton

0 25 50 Miles
0 25 50 Kilometers

◉ Cities with more
   than 500,000 people
• City or town
▲ Mountain
   peak or hill

Read a State Map

Use the state map of Ohio on page 18 to answer these questions.

1. Name the five states that border Ohio.

2. Use the scale to find out how far the state capital is from Cleveland.

3. In which direction would you travel to get from Akron to Columbus?

4. Find Mansfield on the map. What is the name of the town 25 miles due south of Mansfield?

5. Ohio has cities with names that begin with letters from A–Z. Name one city that begins with an "A" and one that begins with a "Z."

6. If you measure across Lake Erie, how far is Toledo from the Canadian border?

7. Orville Wright, the famous aviation pioneer, was born in Dayton. Find his birthplace on the map. How far is Dayton from Cincinnati?

8. What is the name of the river that runs along Ohio's southern border?

TEST TIP

To remember the names of the five Great Lakes, remember HOMES: **H**uron **O**ntario **M**ichigan **E**rie **S**uperior

HOW TO

Read a Continent Map

The Big Picture

Areas of land come in every size —from very small to very, very large. There are tiny islands located in the Pacific Ocean, and there are huge areas of land located mainly in the northern hemisphere. There are general names given to the areas of land and water in the world. Bodies of water can be called *rivers, lakes,* or *oceans;* and areas of land can be called *islands, countries,* or *continents.*

Satellite image of planet Earth, showing oceans and continents

The largest areas of water on Earth are called oceans. The largest areas of land on Earth are called **continents.** Certain features of nature such as mountains and oceans determine continental boundaries. There are seven continents and four oceans on Earth. The names of the seven continents are Asia, Africa, North America, South America, Antarctica, Europe, and Australia.

This world map shows the locations of the oceans and continents. You can read and study the map from top to bottom or from left to right.

Seven Continents of the World

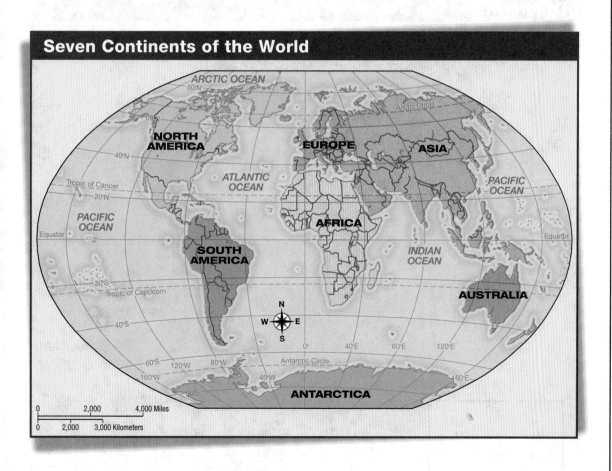

Continents are usually large, unbroken masses of land. Every continent on Earth has a variety of landforms. **Landforms** are natural features on the surface of Earth, both above and below water. For example, **deserts** are dry areas where few plants and animals live. **Mountains** are high, sloping, often rocky landforms. **Valleys** are lower areas near mountains and hills. **Plains** are large, flat areas. **Islands** are areas of land surrounded by water, and are smaller than continents. These are just a few of the many types of landforms.

The map below is a physical map of Africa, showing only natural features.

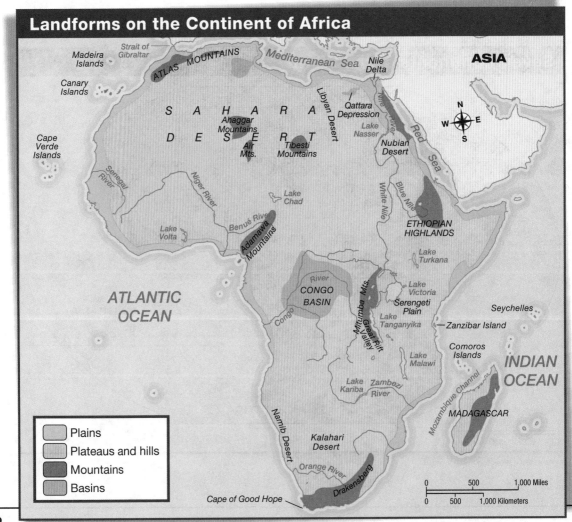

Landforms on the Continent of Africa

Madeira Islands
Strait of Gibraltar
ATLAS MOUNTAINS
Mediterranean Sea
Nile Delta
ASIA

Canary Islands

S A H A R A   Libyan Desert
Qattara Depression

Cape Verde Islands

D E S E R T
Ahaggar Mountains
Air Mts.
Tibesti Mountains
Lake Nasser
Nubian Desert

N W E S
Red Sea

Senegal River
Niger River
Lake Chad
White Nile
Blue Nile

Lake Volta
Benué River
Adamawa Mountains

ETHIOPIAN HIGHLANDS

Lake Turkana

ATLANTIC OCEAN

River
CONGO BASIN
Congo
Mitumba Mts.
Great Rift Valley
Lake Victoria
Serengeti Plain
Lake Tanganyika
Zanzibar Island

Seychelles

Comoros Islands

INDIAN OCEAN

Lake Malawi

Lake Kariba
Zambezi River

Mozambique Channel

MADAGASCAR

Namib Desert
Kalahari Desert

Orange River
Drakensberg
Cape of Good Hope

Plains
Plateaus and hills
Mountains
Basins

0   500   1,000 Miles
0   500   1,000 Kilometers

Country is a political term meaning nation or independent territory. There can be many countries on a single continent. Countries have boundaries made by people. When used on maps, **boundaries** are imaginary lines that show how land is divided into cities, states, or countries. Colors are often used on maps to highlight different states or countries. When more than one country is on a continent, colors are helpful in telling the countries apart.

Look at the political map below to see the many countries on the continent of Africa.

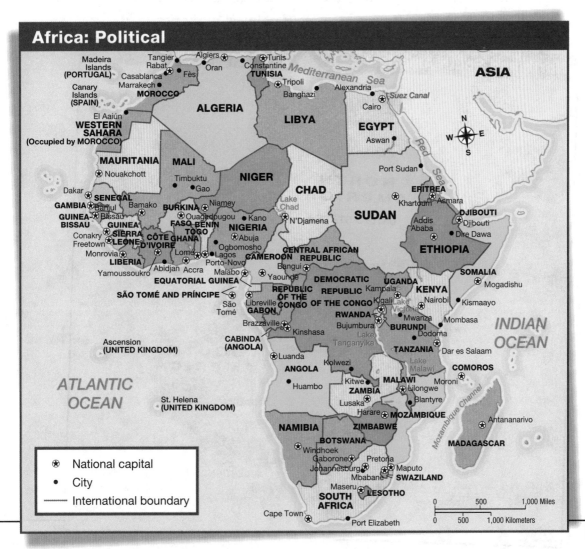

Africa: Political

Madeira Islands (PORTUGAL)
Canary Islands (SPAIN)

Tangier
Rabat
Casablanca
Marrakech
Fès
MOROCCO

Algiers
Oran
Constantine
TUNISIA
Tunis
Tripoli
Banghazi
Alexandria
Cairo
Suez Canal

Mediterranean Sea

ASIA

El Aaiún
WESTERN SAHARA
(Occupied by MOROCCO)

ALGERIA

LIBYA

EGYPT
Aswan

Red Sea

MAURITANIA
Nouakchott

MALI
Timbuktu
Gao

NIGER
Niamey

CHAD
Lake Chad
N'Djamena

Port Sudan

ERITREA
Khartoum
Asmara

SUDAN

Addis Ababa
Djibouti
DJIBOUTI
Dire Dawa

Dakar
SENEGAL
GAMBIA Banjul
GUINEA BISSAU Bissau
GUINEA
Conakry
Freetown
SIERRA LEONE
Monrovia
LIBERIA
Yamoussoukro

Bamako
BURKINA FASO
Ouagadougou
Kano
BENIN
TOGO
CÔTE D'IVOIRE
GHANA
Abidjan
Accra
Lomé
Porto-Novo
NIGERIA
Abuja
Ogbomosho
Lagos
Malabo

CENTRAL AFRICAN REPUBLIC
Bangui

ETHIOPIA

CAMEROON
Yaoundé

SOMALIA
Mogadishu

EQUATORIAL GUINEA
SÃO TOMÉ AND PRÍNCIPE
São Tomé
GABON
Libreville

DEMOCRATIC REPUBLIC OF THE CONGO
REPUBLIC OF THE CONGO
Brazzaville
Kinshasa

UGANDA
Kampala
Kigali
RWANDA
Bujumbura
BURUNDI

KENYA
Nairobi
Lake Victoria
Mwanza
Dodoma

Kismaayo
Mombasa

INDIAN OCEAN

Ascension (UNITED KINGDOM)

CABINDA (ANGOLA)
Luanda

ANGOLA
Huambo

Kolwezi
Kitwe
Lusaka
ZAMBIA

Lake Tanganyika
TANZANIA
Dar es Salaam

Lake Malawi
MALAWI
Lilongwe
Blantyre

COMOROS
Moroni

ATLANTIC OCEAN

St. Helena (UNITED KINGDOM)

Harare
MOZAMBIQUE

Mozambique Channel

Antananarivo

NAMIBIA
Windhoek

ZIMBABWE

BOTSWANA
Gaborone
Johannesburg
Pretoria
Maputo
Mbabane
SWAZILAND

MADAGASCAR

Maseru
LESOTHO
SOUTH AFRICA
Cape Town
Port Elizabeth

⊛ National capital
• City
—— International boundary

0   500   1,000 Miles
0   500   1,000 Kilometers

The United States often is called *America*. In this case, "America" is just a short way to say the name of the country "The United States of America." There are really two continents called "the Americas"— North America and South America. North America includes the countries of Canada, the United States, and Mexico. South America includes the countries of Colombia, Venezuela, Brazil, Argentina, and many others. On a narrower area called a *land bridge* between these two continents are the seven countries of Central America. Central America is usually considered part of the North American continent. Between countries lie natural boundaries like mountain ranges, as well as the human-made boundaries that outline political territories.

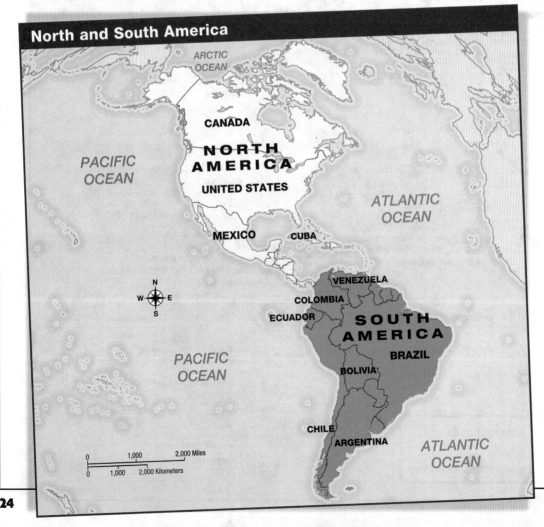

North and South America

Read a Continent Map

Use the continent maps on pages 20–24 to answer the following questions.

1. What is the name of the continent to the north of Africa?

2. Which of the seven continents is the largest?

3. What is the name of the largest desert on the African continent?

4. What is the name of the large lake northwest of the Serengeti Plain?

5. What is the name of the country located on the southern tip of Africa?

6. Chad and Sudan are located in central Africa. How can you tell that Chad and Sudan are two separate countries?

7. North and South America are between which two oceans?

8. Name four countries located on the South American continent.

TEST TIP	When a test asks questions about a continent map, look at the whole map, not just one part of it.

Skill 5

HOW TO

Read a Grid Map

X Marks the Spot

What does "X marks the spot" mean? An **X** drawn on a map pinpoints a location. In order to tell the exact spot where a place is located, maps and globes use grids of imaginary lines. One set of lines runs east and west, and another set of lines runs north and south. The lines crisscross each other and divide the map into squares.

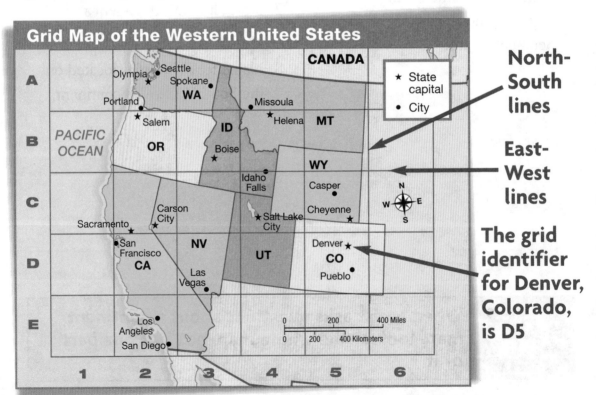

Grid Map of the Western United States

North-South lines

East-West lines

The grid identifier for Denver, Colorado, is D5

A **grid map** uses sets of crisscrossing lines to divide a map into squares. Grid maps use letters and numbers to identify the squares. The letters and numbers are printed across the top or bottom of the grid, and down one or both sides. The letter and number combination used to identify a place on a grid is called a **grid identifier.** Grid identifiers are written letter first, then number.

Not all grid maps show lines on the map. Sometimes, the letters and numbers are shown on the edges of the grid map, and you have to imagine the lines.

To find the grid identifier for a place, all you have to do is use your fingers to go straight out to the sides and the top of the map. Place both of your fingers on the map location.

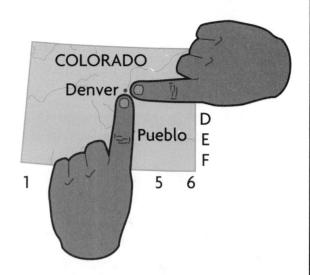

Move one finger straight toward the letters at the edge of the map. Move the other finger straight toward the numbers at the other edge of the map. When both fingers are on or near a letter or number, stop. Write down the closest letter and number to each finger.

You can also find a location on a grid map with just the grid identifier number. Find the letter and the number from the grid identifier on the edges of your grid map. Start out with one finger on the letter on the grid, and the other finger on the number. Move both fingers straight in toward the map until they touch. The spot where your fingers meet will mark the location you want.

> **TIP** When using a grid map to find the location of a place, look for the **closest** grid identifier. Some locations will not be at the exact intersection of two lines on the grid.

Grid maps can be used to show any area of the world. The map below is a grid map of the state of Colorado.

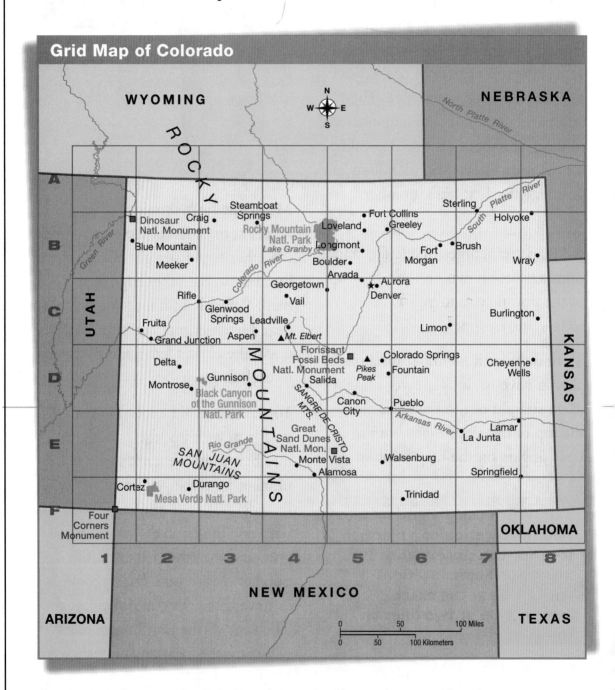

Grid Map of Colorado

WYOMING

NEBRASKA

ROCKY

N
W · E
S

A

B

Dinosaur Natl. Monument
Craig
Steamboat Springs
Rocky Mountain Natl. Park
Lake Granby
Loveland
Longmont
Fort Collins
Greeley
Sterling
Platte River
South Platte
Holyoke
North Platte River

Blue Mountain
Fort Morgan
Brush
Wray

Meeker
Boulder
Arvada

C

Rifle
Georgetown
Aurora
Denver
Burlington

Fruita
Glenwood Springs
Leadville
Vail
Limon

Grand Junction
Aspen
Mt. Elbert

UTAH

D

Delta
Florissant Fossil Beds Natl. Monument
Colorado Springs
Cheyenne Wells

Montrose
Gunnison
Salida
Pikes Peak
Fountain

Black Canyon of the Gunnison Natl. Park
Canon City
Pueblo
Arkansas River
Lamar
La Junta

MOUNTAINS

KANSAS

E

Great Sand Dunes Natl. Mon.
Monte Vista
Alamosa
Walsenburg
Springfield

SAN JUAN MOUNTAINS
Rio Grande
SANGRE DE CRISTO MTS.

Cortez
Durango
Trinidad

Mesa Verde Natl. Park

F

Four Corners Monument

OKLAHOMA

1   2   3   4   5   6   7   8

NEW MEXICO

ARIZONA

TEXAS

0   50   100 Miles
0   50   100 Kilometers

Read a Grid Map

Use the grid map of Colorado on page 28 to answer these questions.

1. What is the grid identifier for the city of Aspen, Colorado?

2. How would you tell someone to find Fort Morgan on the grid map?

3. The highest point in Colorado is Mount Elbert. It is 14,433 feet high. What is the grid location for Mount Elbert?

4. What city is found at F6 on the map?

5. What is the name of the national park found at F2 on the map?

6. The southwest corner of the state is known as "Four Corners." It is the only point in the United States where four states touch at one location. What is the grid identifier for this point?

7. Does the Rio Grande pass through grid location D7?

8. At what grid location are Boulder, Longmont, Loveland, Fort Collins, and Greeley all found?

TEST TIP

Sometimes a test will ask questions about locations on a grid map. Use a ruler or the straight edge of a piece of paper to help you find exact points on a grid map.

HOW TO

Read a Historical Map

Early American History in Maps

Words and photographs in history books tell about important events of the past. Maps can add details to the stories that words and pictures tell. They show the places where certain events happened and the order in which events occurred. Maps present their own special pictures of history.

A **historical map** is a map that shows the features, boundaries, or events of a region's past. Historical maps can show how regions and countries have changed over time. Historical maps help explain the events of history.

When reading a historical map, first read the map title to learn what area and what time period are being shown.

Pay close attention to the symbols used on the map by reading the legend to find their meanings.

Compare the map to other historical maps of the same area during different time periods to study changes over time. You might also want to compare the historical map to a present-day map of the area. This can help you see what has changed and what has stayed the same.

The map on the next page shows details that can help you understand the text below it.

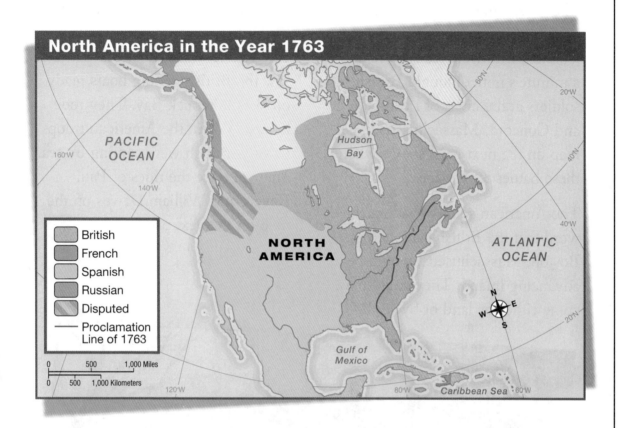

North America in the Year 1763

PACIFIC OCEAN

160°W

140°W

Hudson Bay

60°N

20°W

40°N

40°W

NORTH AMERICA

ATLANTIC OCEAN

40°N

Legend:
- British
- French
- Spanish
- Russian
- Disputed
- Proclamation Line of 1763

0   500   1,000 Miles
0   500   1,000 Kilometers

120°W

Gulf of Mexico

80°W

Caribbean Sea

60°W

20°N

European colonists had been coming to North America since before 1600. The British had thirteen colonies along the east coast by 1732, but much of the continent still belonged to the French.

After the French and Indian War ended in 1763, the British controlled all of the land east of the Mississippi River. Spain owned the land between the Mississippi River and the Rocky Mountains. The remaining northwestern territory was unexplored.

TIP On historical maps, titles often include dates. Reading the title of a map first will help you place the country or region shown on the map in the correct time period.

The Revolutionary War began in 1775, when America's Minutemen (soldiers who were ready to march at a minute's notice) fought British soldiers at the cities of Lexington and Concord, Massachusetts. The map on the next page shows where these battles took place.

The American soldiers had received word that the British stationed in Boston, Massachusetts, would be advancing inland. They could have come either by land or by sea.

American soldiers were prepared for the British advance because Paul Revere and other American patriots saw the British getting boats ready on Boston's Back Bay. They rode horses to warn the American troops that the British were coming by sea. You can trace the rides of Paul Revere and William Dawes on the map on the next page.

Paul Revere on his famous ride

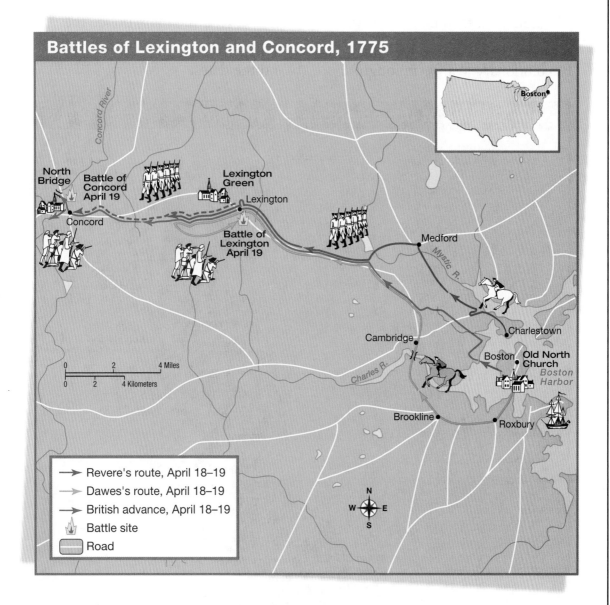

Battles of Lexington and Concord, 1775

North Bridge

Battle of Concord April 19

Lexington Green

Lexington

Concord

Battle of Lexington April 19

Medford

Mystic R.

Concord River

Cambridge

Charles R.

Charlestown

Boston   Old North Church

Boston Harbor

Brookline

Roxbury

Boston

0   2   4 Miles

0   2   4 Kilometers

→ Revere's route, April 18–19

→ Dawes's route, April 18–19

→ British advance, April 18–19

⚑ Battle site

▭ Road

N W E S

The historical map above shows an area that is today the state of Massachusetts. The map features help explain what happened at Lexington and Concord in 1775.

The battles that took place at Lexington and at Concord were the first major conflicts of the Revolutionary War.

The historical map below shows where major battles of the Revolutionary War were fought.

As you read the map, notice the map features, the names of battles, and the dates.

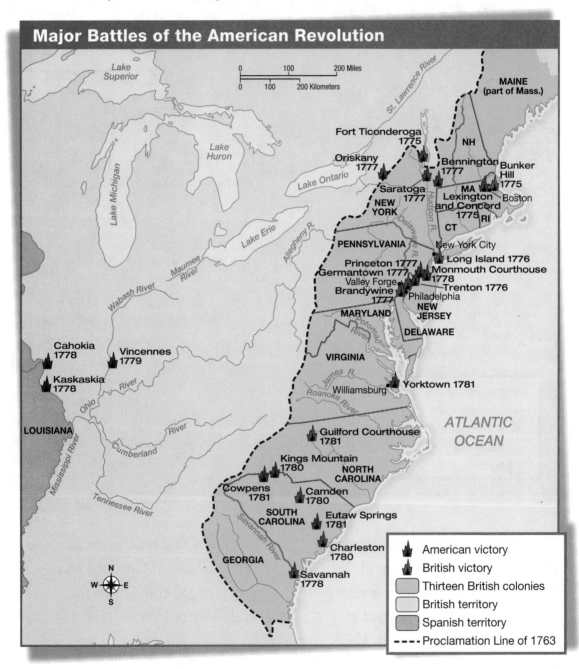

Major Battles of the American Revolution

Lake Superior

0   100   200 Miles
0   100   200 Kilometers

St. Lawrence River

MAINE
(part of Mass.)

Lake Huron

Lake Michigan

Fort Ticonderoga 1775

NH

Oriskany 1777

Bennington 1777

Bunker Hill 1775

Lake Ontario

Saratoga 1777

Hudson R.

MA

Lexington and Concord 1775

Boston

NEW YORK

RI

Lake Erie

Allegheny R.

Delaware R.

CT

Maumee River

PENNSYLVANIA

New York City

Long Island 1776

Wabash River

Princeton 1777
Germantown 1777
Valley Forge
Brandywine 1777

Monmouth Courthouse 1778

Trenton 1776

Philadelphia

NEW JERSEY

MARYLAND

DELAWARE

Cahokia 1778

Vincennes 1779

Potomac River

VIRGINIA

Kaskaskia 1778

River

James R.

Yorktown 1781

Ohio

Williamsburg

Roanoke River

ATLANTIC OCEAN

LOUISIANA

Cumberland River

Mississippi River

Guilford Courthouse 1781

Tennessee River

Kings Mountain 1780

NORTH CAROLINA

Cowpens 1781

Camden 1780

SOUTH CAROLINA

Eutaw Springs 1781

N
W   E
S

Savannah River

Charleston 1780

GEORGIA

Savannah 1778

American victory
British victory
Thirteen British colonies
British territory
Spanish territory
Proclamation Line of 1763

Read a Historical Map

Use the maps on pages 33 and 34 to answer the following questions about the Revolutionary War.

1. On the map on page 33, what do the red lines and arrows represent?

2. Use the map scale on page 33 to measure the distance of Paul Revere's famous ride.

3. Use the map scale to measure the distance between Trenton, New Jersey, and Concord, Massachusetts, on the map on page 34.

4. On the map on page 34, what symbol shows an American battle victory?

5. How many years did battles continue after the U.S. Congress adopted the Declaration of Independence on July 4, 1776?

6. In what present-day state was the battle of Camden fought?

7. Were more battles fought north or south of the Potomac River?

8. In what year did the battle of Yorktown take place?

TEST TIP — A test may ask you to use the symbols on a map to answer questions. Always study a map's legend, or key, to understand the meaning of symbols on the map.

Skill 7

HOW TO

Read a Cultural Map

Native American Lands

All of the land that is now the United States was once home to great nations of Native Americans. Native American groups numbered in the hundreds when Columbus first set foot on the continent of North America. Each of these groups had their own traditions, languages, and beliefs — their own culture.

Culture refers to the customs, arts, beliefs, and other traits shared by groups of people. A **cultural map** is a map that shows the place or places where different social groups live or have lived. Cultural maps can be historical maps, showing where certain social groups lived in years past. Cultural maps can also be maps that show the regions where these same groups or other groups live today. Cultural maps are used by historians to study the events of history, and by anthropologists who study the peoples who have lived on Earth. Cultural maps also are used by students like you, who want to know more about the world.

There are two important steps that will help you read and understand a cultural map. First, look closely at the map title. The map title tells you what is being shown on the map. Map titles often give the time period and the names of events or peoples represented on the map. Second, notice the symbols and/or colors used on the map. If the map has a legend, study it to find out what these colors and symbols represent.

Before studying a cultural map, knowing the general history of the region is often helpful.

The cultural map below shows how the territory of the United States expanded during the 1800s. The United States of America began, developed, and expanded on the lands of Native American peoples. These lands had been native peoples' homes for thousands of years. From the seventeenth through the nineteenth centuries, the British, Dutch, French, and Spanish competed for land in North America. Native Americans were caught in the middle of these struggles for land.

> **TIP** The word **nation** can mean a community of people living together in a common region, or it can refer to the region itself.

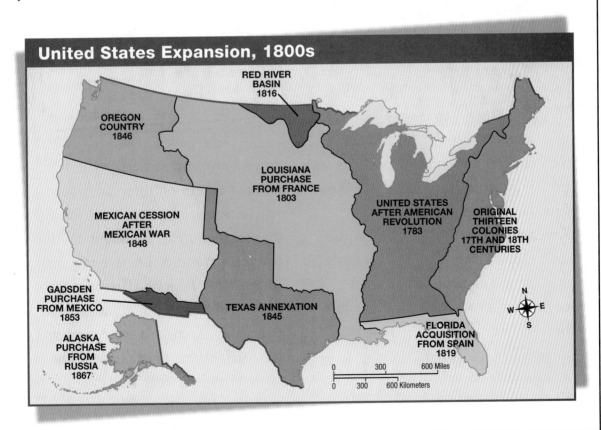

United States Expansion, 1800s

RED RIVER BASIN 1816

OREGON COUNTRY 1846

LOUISIANA PURCHASE FROM FRANCE 1803

UNITED STATES AFTER AMERICAN REVOLUTION 1783

ORIGINAL THIRTEEN COLONIES 17TH AND 18TH CENTURIES

MEXICAN CESSION AFTER MEXICAN WAR 1848

GADSDEN PURCHASE FROM MEXICO 1853

TEXAS ANNEXATION 1845

FLORIDA ACQUISITION FROM SPAIN 1819

ALASKA PURCHASE FROM RUSSIA 1867

0   300   600 Miles
0   300   600 Kilometers

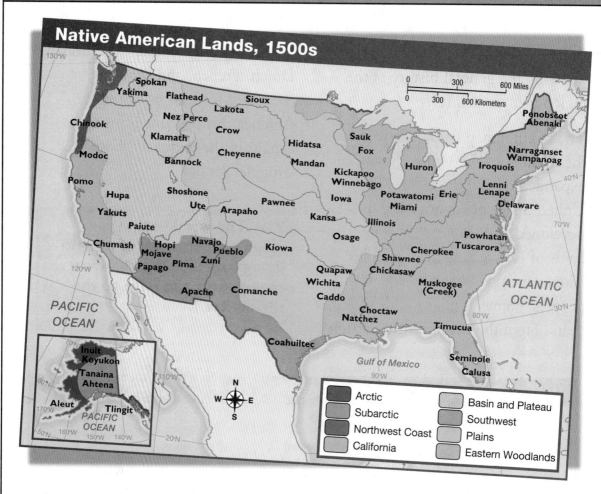

Native American Lands, 1500s

The cultural map on this page shows part of North America in the 1500s. Homelands of many Native American groups are shown on the map. You already know from your studies of American history that during the 1500s, European settlers had not yet claimed much of this land.

After European settlers began forcing native peoples off their land, the native peoples had to live in smaller and smaller areas. Different cultural groups were forced to live together in the same regions. They did not always succeed in living together peaceably. Some Native Americans have called this time period "The Four-Hundred-Year War."

When European settlers began moving onto Native American lands in the 1800s, the U.S. government wanted to make room for them. The Indian Removal Act of 1830 allowed President Andrew Jackson to "relocate" the Native American groups living east of the Mississippi River. These peoples were moved west to lands in the present-day state of Oklahoma.

Whole nations such as the Cherokee, the Choctaw, the Creek,

The Great Serpent Mound in Ohio was made by Native Americans.

and the Seminole were relocated. Many Native Americans were marched along what the Cherokee call the "Trail of Tears." They were forced to leave lands that had been home to their families for generations. They knew how to make use of the natural resources and live in harmony with nature, but they did not know what they would find in the new "Indian Territory" lands. The kinds of homes they built, the clothes they made, their language, and the foods they ate depended on the natural world around them. Being forced to move to unknown territory would change their entire way of life.

Read the cultural map below. The map shows the Native American groups that were moved from their homelands to new regions in the west from 1830 to 1855.

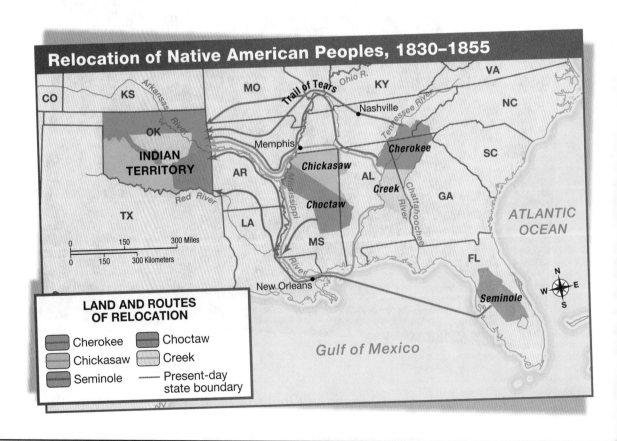

Relocation of Native American Peoples, 1830–1855

LAND AND ROUTES OF RELOCATION
- Cherokee
- Chickasaw
- Seminole
- Choctaw
- Creek
- Present-day state boundary

Read a Cultural Map

Use the cultural map on page 40 to answer the following questions.

1. How many groups are shown on the map?

2. Use the compass rose to tell in which direction the Creeks were moved from what today is the state of Alabama.

3. Name two rivers that the Native Americans crossed.

4. Where did the Seminole live before their 1832 removal?

5. Which group traveled the farthest?

6. How long is the time period shown on the map on page 40?

7. What color is used on the map for the Choctaw?

8. What is the name of the river at the southern border of Indian Territory?

9. Which group traveled the northernmost route?

10. In which present-day state were the Native Americans' new lands located?

TEST TIP When a test asks questions about a cultural map, pay careful attention to the questions and answer choices. These questions will be different from the questions about a physical or political map.

Skill 8
HOW TO
Read a Road Map

Pacific Coast Highway

How would you number the more than 400,000 miles of highways that snake around and across the land, rivers, and mountains of the United States? Some highways have a state number, some have a U.S. number, and some have both. In the 1920s, the government officially assigned odd numbers to north-south highways and even numbers to east-west highways. The most important north-south route at the time was along the Atlantic Coast. This route was named U.S. Highway 1. The most famous Highway 1, though, is a state highway 3,000 miles away in California.

Big Sur, California

Along the beautiful, rugged coast of California, there is another Highway 1 that follows the coastline for over 600 miles. This is a state highway that is better known as the Pacific Coast Highway. You can find Highway 1 on a California road map. A **road map** is a map that shows the streets and highways in a city, state, province or country, as well as the important cities, national parks, and other interesting sights.

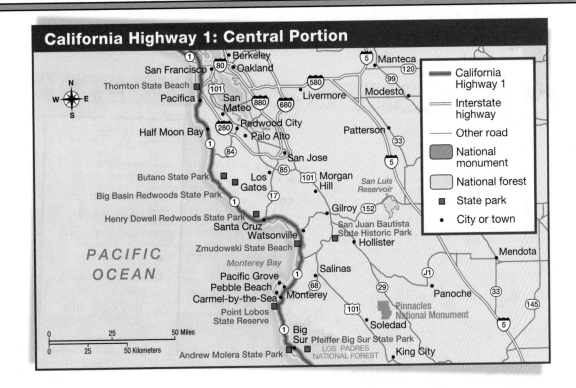

California Highway 1: Central Portion

Taking a good road map along on a trip allows you to find the best route to your destination.

The scale on a road map can be used to tell the driving distance between locations. The map above, for example, shows a portion of the Pacific Coast Highway from San Francisco to Big Sur. Using the map scale as a guide, you will find that there are about 130 miles between the two places.

You can use the map scale to help figure out how long it will take to drive from one place to another. First measure the distance using the scale, then divide that number by the speed at which you will travel. This will give you an estimated driving time. For example, if the distance is 90 miles and you plan to travel at about 45 miles per hour, the trip will take about two hours (90 ÷ 45 = 2).

Highway 1 is a scenic highway. A **scenic highway** is a roadway that allows travelers to see the natural beauty of areas around the roadway.

Read the road map of Highway 1 below. Use the legend for help
reading symbols.

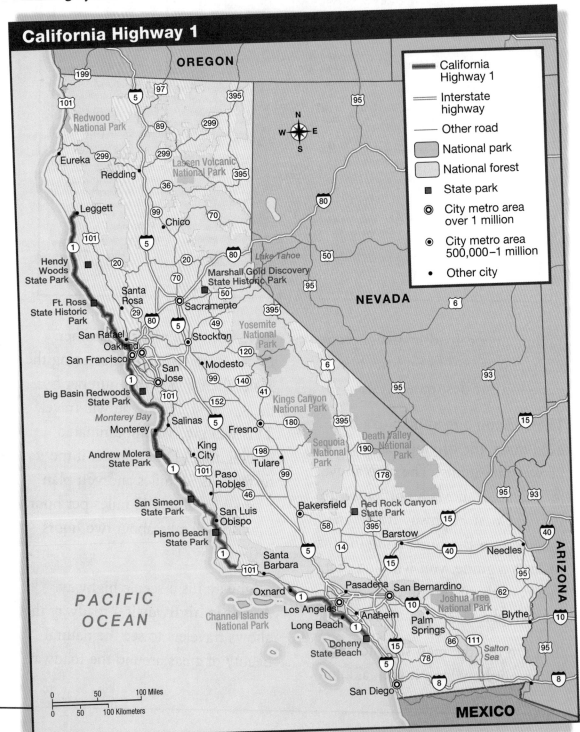

California Highway 1

OREGON

NEVADA

ARIZONA

PACIFIC
OCEAN

MEXICO

Legend:
- California Highway 1
- Interstate highway
- Other road
- National park
- National forest
- State park
- City metro area over 1 million
- City metro area 500,000–1 million
- Other city

Redwood National Park
Eureka
Redding
Lassen Volcanic National Park
Leggett
Chico
Hendy Woods State Park
Santa Rosa
Ft. Ross State Historic Park
Marshall Gold Discovery State Historic Park
Sacramento
San Rafael
Oakland
Stockton
Yosemite National Park
San Francisco
Modesto
San Jose
Big Basin Redwoods State Park
Monterey Bay
Monterey
Salinas
Fresno
Kings Canyon National Park
King City
Tulare
Sequoia National Park
Andrew Molera State Park
Paso Robles
San Simeon State Park
San Luis Obispo
Bakersfield
Red Rock Canyon State Park
Pismo Beach State Park
Barstow
Santa Barbara
Needles
Oxnard
Pasadena
San Bernardino
Joshua Tree National Park
Los Angeles
Anaheim
Channel Islands National Park
Long Beach
Palm Springs
Blythe
Doheny State Beach
Salton Sea
San Diego

Lake Tahoe
Death Valley National Park

0   50   100 Miles
0   50   100 Kilometers

USE THIS SKILL

Read a Road Map

Use the road map on page 44 to answer these questions.

1. What other U.S. highway runs roughly north and south in California like State Highway 1?

2. What color line represents an interstate highway on the map?

3. Use the scale to estimate the distance from San Francisco to Andrew Molera State Park.

4. What symbol represents a state park on the map?

5. Is Los Angeles north or south of San Diego?

6. Does Highway 1 go through the city of Eureka?

7. What symbol on the map represents cities with populations under 500,000 people?

8. Use the scale to estimate the distance across Monterey Bay, from Santa Cruz to Monterey.

TEST TIP

When a test asks questions about the highways on a road map, study the map legend (or key) to make sure that you know the difference between the symbol for a U.S. highway sign and a state highway sign.

HOW TO

Read a Product Map

Yankee Traders

Before railroads and trucks carried goods across the United States, peddlers—or traders—drove their wagons from town to town selling all kinds of handmade items. When machines replaced people as the makers of most products, New England became a manufacturing region.

Various goods are produced or manufactured in different regions of the United States and in other countries of the world. Reading about what is produced in various regions is one way of learning about the economy and resources of a country. A country's **economy** is the way it makes and uses money, products, and services. Looking at a product map can also give a lot of information about a country's economy and resources.

A **product map** shows the goods, or products, that are made or grown in a certain area. A product map is a kind of special-purpose map called a thematic map. **Thematic maps** focus on one main theme, or subject. The map on the facing page is a thematic map that shows where goods are made and where food is grown in the United States.

The nation's railroads, airlines, and highways form a cross-country transportation system. This system allows manufacturers to quickly and easily ship their products north, south, east, west, and anywhere in between.

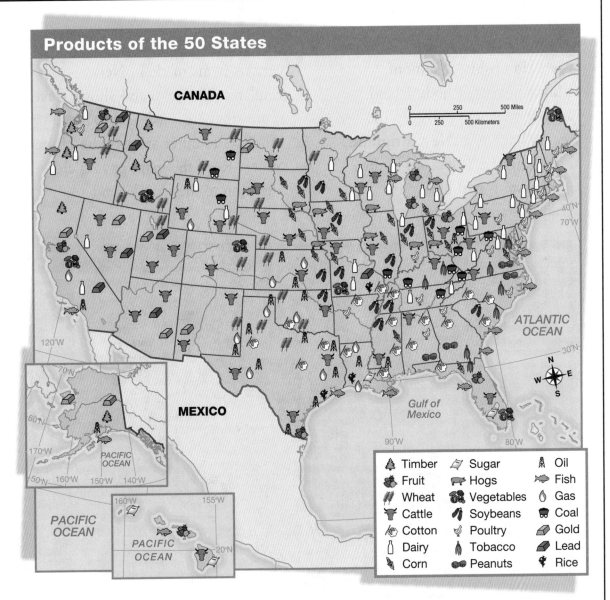

Products of the 50 States

Legend:

Timber	Sugar	Oil
Fruit	Hogs	Fish
Wheat	Vegetables	Gas
Cattle	Soybeans	Coal
Cotton	Poultry	Gold
Dairy	Tobacco	Lead
Corn	Peanuts	Rice

This system of selling and transporting allows people in cities to buy fresh eggs, meat, and dairy products. People who live in northern climates can buy oranges and fresh vegetables from the south and the west at any time of year. No matter where you live, you can buy grapes from California and have maple syrup from Vermont on your pancakes.

The six states of Maine, New Hampshire, Vermont, Massachusetts, Rhode Island, and Connecticut make up the region known as **New England.** New England is located in the northeastern part of the United States.

The product map below shows various items made in New England. The map also shows travel routes that are used to ship these products to other areas of the United States. Read the map, paying close attention to the map legend.

Products of New England

CANADA

MAINE

Bangor

VERMONT
Burlington

NEW HAMPSHIRE

Portland

ATLANTIC OCEAN

NY

Manchester

MASSACHUSETTS

Boston

Springfield

Hartford

Providence

CONNECTICUT RHODE ISLAND

Bridgeport

PA

NJ

🍯	Maple syrup
⊚	Machinery
✗	Silverware
🐄	Dairy
◣	Granite
●	Cranberries
🐟	Fish
🌲	Timber
💻	Electronic equipment

0 50 100 Miles
0 50 100 Kilometers

N NE
NW E
W SE
SW S

Read a Product Map

Use the map on page 48 to answer the following questions.

1. What are two products made in Connecticut?

2. Name one state in New England where fish is not a main good.

3. Timber is wood that is used for building. Which state on this map produces timber?

4. By what route could cranberries be shipped from Massachusetts to Maine?

5. Use the compass rose to tell in which direction lobsters from Maine would be shipped to Vermont.

6. Name one state where electronic equipment is made.

7. Use the scale to measure the distance that milk from Vermont would have to be shipped to get to Providence, Rhode Island.

8. Are the U.S. interstate highways that run north and south odd numbers or even numbers? What about the east-west interstates?

TEST TIP

When a test asks questions about a product map or other picture map, study the map legend carefully. The same symbol may represent different things on different maps. Taking time to study the symbols will help you to answer test questions correctly.

Skill 10

HOW TO

Read a Climate Map

Weather Report

What's the difference between the weather and the climate? If you look outside, you can observe the sunny or snowy weather. You can see the sun and the rain, and you can feel the heat and the cold. Weather is a condition you can see and feel, but you can't "see" the climate. **Climate** is the term used to describe the average weather conditions of a region over a period of time, such as a year. To understand climate, you have to check temperatures and measure wind speed and rainfall over time.

Many things influence climate. An area's climate is affected by oceans and mountains, by how far above sea level it is, and most importantly, by its *latitude*, or distance from the equator.

A **climate map** gives information about an area's weather patterns using pictures. A climate map is a special-purpose, or thematic, map. A **thematic map** shows information about one theme, or subject.

Climate maps use colors and lines to show differences in temperature and rain, hail, sleet, and snow in a region. Some climate maps show only wind direction or temperature. Arrows and lines are often used to show wind direction on climate maps. Temperature is sometimes shown by different colors or patterns on maps. Other maps give temperature and seasonal information based on climate regions. Some climate maps, like the one below, show the yearly amount of rain or snow in different areas. Notice that the legend shows how different colors are used for various amounts of rain or snow.

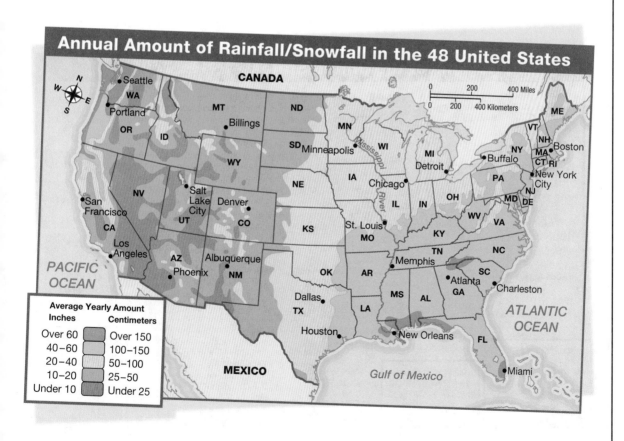

Annual Amount of Rainfall/Snowfall in the 48 United States

Average Yearly Amount

Inches	Centimeters
Over 60	Over 150
40–60	100–150
20–40	50–100
10–20	25–50
Under 10	Under 25

There are five general kinds of climate regions on Earth. **Tropical** regions have warm temperatures and a lot of rainfall. Hawaii is a tropical region that is close to the equator.

Most of the United States is in the **midlatitude** region. These areas are shown by shades of purple on the map. Some midlatitude regions have warm, humid summers and mild winters (like the southwestern United States); and other areas have warm summers and cold winters (like the Northeast and the Midwest).

Dry regions, like those west of the Rocky Mountains, have very little rainfall or snowfall. Some dry regions are deserts, like the area east of Los Angeles, California. Alaska is in a **high latitude** climate region, where summers are very short. **Highland** areas are high, mountainous regions.

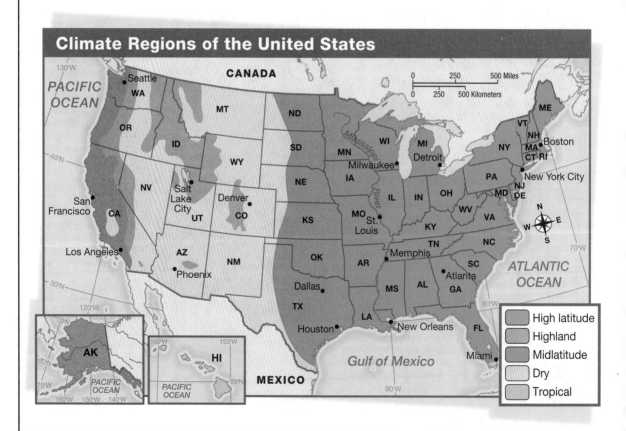

Climate Regions of the United States

Read a Climate Map

Use the climate map on page 52 to answer the following questions.

1. What areas of the continental United States have tropical climates?

2. Into what climate region does Alaska fall?

3. Use the scale to estimate the distance from the highland area in Arizona to the highland area in Colorado.

4. What color is used on the map to represent tropical climate regions?

5. Which states have the driest climates?

6. Are there any regions in the continental United States that have the same type of climate as Hawaii?

7. What climate region is represented by the color purple on the map?

8. Which states include more than two climate regions?

TEST TIP When a test asks you to answer questions about a climate map, read the legend carefully. Don't try to answer the questions using information you remember from other sources.

Reading and Thinking Skills

Skill 11

HOW TO

Classify

The Road to Freedom

What do you think of when you hear the word "Conductor"? Some people think of a train conductor or the conductor of an orchestra. But to Harriet Tubman, being a conductor on the Underground Railroad meant risking her life to help African Americans escape slavery. In the ten years between 1850 and 1860, she led about 300 people on secret voyages north toward freedom.

The "Underground Railroad" was the name given to secret routes between the "slave" states of the southern United States and the "free" states of the North. It was not a real railroad, but a secret network of hiding places, safe houses, and helpful people stretching for

Harriet Tubman, 1860s

hundreds of miles. Slaves hoping for better lives as free men and women traveled north on foot, following "conductors" like Harriet Tubman who knew the way. They often traveled at night, hiding in the barns, attics, or cellars of safe houses.

You can understand and remember historical information better if you organize it in your mind. Classifying information is one way to organize it. When you **classify,** you group objects, people, events, actions, or ideas based on something they have in common.

STEPS IN Classifying

1 Choose the Information

You can classify any kind of information. People can be classified by where they live, when they were born, or what they do. Things can be classified by their size, shape, or color. Events can be classified as happening before or after other events. To get started, decide what you want to classify and why.

2 Examine the Details

Focus on one important quality of the items you want to classify. For example, if you are grouping events in American history, you could classify them as before or after the Civil War. Words such as *before, after,* and *during* signal **time sequence,** or the order in which events took place. These words can help you classify. You can also use words such as *yesterday, today, tomorrow, last week,* and *next year* to classify events by time sequence.

3 Record the Information

Keep track of your classification by making lists, diagrams, or charts. These will help make the information you have classified easy to understand.

Before Escaping	After Escaping
Hard work on plantation	Hard work at a factory
Not paid for work	Paid each week
Family split up, living on different plantations	Family is safe and living together

Read the following passage. Notice how events are classified as before and after slavery.

Harriet Tubman's Secret Journey

After → *Harriet Tubman crouched in the woods, listening for the barking of the slave catchers' dogs. After dark, it would be safe to start moving again. Hiding by day and traveling by night, Tubman reached the home*

After → *of a woman who helped runaway slaves.*

Before she escaped from slavery in

Before → *Maryland, Tubman had heard that her owner was going to sell her. After escaping, she took great risks to travel north*

After → *toward Pennsylvania.*

Tubman had grown up in a close, loving

Before → *family. In Pennsylvania, she thought about* ← After *her family still living in slavery.*

Tubman began working with the Underground Railroad. Returning to slave states at least 15 times, she helped her family and hundreds of others escape to freedom. She freed so many slaves that slave

After → *owners offered forty thousand dollars for her capture. Each time she traveled back to the South, Harriet Tubman risked her life to make a difference in the lives of others.*

Classify

Read the passage below. Classify each sentence as before or after slavery was abolished, or made illegal.

My Life Before and After Slavery

Before I became a free man, I was owned as a slave. I had to work from before sunrise to after sunset, six days a week, with no pay. Slaves on the farm were not given much to eat, so I was always hungry.

I was so unhappy as a slave that I dreamed of freedom night and day. I had secret meetings with other slaves, planning our escape. Then, late one night, we quietly left the farm. With the help of many people along the Underground Railroad, we all made it to freedom in Ohio.

Now it is many years later, and slavery is no more. Times are still hard, but at least we have our freedom. We no longer have to fear being captured and returned to cruel masters. Slavery has been abolished, and America is truly the "Land of the Free."

TEST TIP

On some tests you may need to classify people, events, objects, or ideas in a reading passage. As you read, think about how ideas are related so you can sort them into groups.

Skill 12

HOW TO

Compare and Contrast

Hard Times in the Dust Bowl

History is full of stories about how life was different in the past. For people in the "Dust Bowl" region of the United States in the 1930s, life was full of changes and challenges.

When you think about how people, events, and ideas are similar,

A Dust Bowl farm, 1930s

you are **comparing.** When you think about how they are different, you are **contrasting.** Look for comparisons and contrasts in the following reading.

The Great Plains cover parts of the central United States. This huge area has few trees and long dry periods with no rain. The Great Plains were once covered with grasses growing in fertile topsoil. Then during the 1800s, ranchers began to graze cattle and plant wheat on the plains. The cattle ate much of the grass, leaving the fine soil uncovered. By the year 1930, the plains were so dry and bare that most of the topsoil had been blown away by the wind. People began to call a large area of the Great Plains "The Dust Bowl."

1 Think about Your Topic

Decide what you want to compare and contrast. Are you comparing different times, places, things, cultures, or people? Figure out exactly what your topic will be.

2 Look for Signal Words

Words such as *same, similar, like, both, as, also,* and *too* may signal comparison.

<u>Like</u> the wild grasses, wheat grew well on the Great Plains.

Words such as *unlike, but, more, less, than, better, worse,* and *different* may signal contrast.

<u>Unlike</u> wheat, the wild grasses held the soil in place.

Endings on words, such as *-er* and *-est,* may show contrast.

After years without rain, soil on the plains became dri<u>er</u> than it had ever been before.

3 Look for Similarities and Differences

Even if you do not see any signal words, there may be comparing and contrasting information in the reading.

The cattle ate much of the grass, leaving the fine soil uncovered.

Before Dry Period and Farming	After Dry Period and Farming
Few trees	Few trees
Long dry periods	Long dry periods
Fertile grassland	Cattle ate grass
Wild grasses held soil in place	Wind blew uncovered soil away

Read this history passage and think about how it compares and contrasts the Great Plains before and after the Dust Bowl period.

The Dust Bowl

On the Great Plains, the roots of wild grasses formed a tough mat that held the soil together. From the 1890s through the 1920s, settlers moved in to graze cattle and grow cotton and wheat. **Compares** → Both the cotton and the wheat grew well during rainy years, and both died in dry weather. The 1930s were ← **Contrasts** much drier than the 1920s. Unlike the wild grasses, the wheat could not hold the soil in place during dry years. Both the cotton and the wheat died, leaving the soil uncovered. Then the strong winds picked up the fine soil and carried it away. Clouds of dust swept across the land, burying homes, farms, and livestock.

The Dust Bowl, 1930s

Area of the Dust Bowl

CANADA

MT
ID
WY
UT
CO
AZ
NM
ND
MN
SD
WI
NE
IA
IL
KS
MO
OK
AR
TX
MS
LA
MEXICO

N W E S

0   200   400 Miles
0   200   400 Kilometers

Compare and Contrast

Read the following paragraph about life before and after the Dust Bowl. List four examples of comparing and contrasting.

Before and After the Dust Bowl

Many areas of the Great Plains were once lush farms, but they became a Dust Bowl after the dry years. The soil had given life to crops and livestock, but when the wind picked it up, it became a killer. Violent storms of dust buried crops, animals, and people. Then the Great Plains were like deserts. Farmers could not grow any crops in the dusty ruins of their farmland.

People who had farmed before the Dust Bowl left their land to find different jobs. Some went to work on farms in California. Unlike their farms in the Great Plains, these farms belonged to other people. The U.S. government was able to help some Dust Bowl farmers, but many others lost their farms, their money, and their way of life.

TEST TIP

Some tests may ask you to compare and contrast people, events, or ideas. First identify the items you should compare or contrast. Then look for similarities and differences.

Skill 13

Determine Cause and Effect

Causes of the Revolutionary War

Have you ever wondered what events led to the American Revolutionary War? Have you thought about what might have happened to make Americans start fighting the British? If you look for causes and effects as you read history, you will learn why events happened.

Something that makes another thing happen is a **cause.** What happens as a result of a cause is an **effect.** Look for causes and effects in the following reading.

In the mid-1700s, more and more European people began leaving their home countries. These people hoped to find new opportunities and better lives in a new land. Some Europeans wanted to live in America, so they settled in the American colonies. A colony is an area controlled by another country. The colonies were ruled by the British, since they were settled on lands claimed by Britain. People in the colonies became unhappy because they thought British laws were unfair.

Use the steps on the next page to help you determine cause and effect.

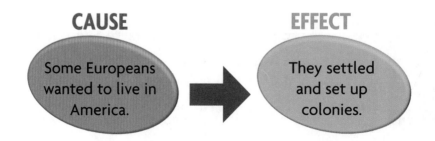

CAUSE

Some Europeans wanted to live in America.

EFFECT

They settled and set up colonies.

STEPS IN Determining Cause and Effect

1 Look for Cue Words

Cue words may signal a cause or effect.

Cue words such as *because,* *since,* and *caused by* may be followed by a cause.

People in the colonies became unhappy with British rulers <u>because</u> they thought they were treated unfairly.

Cue words such as *so,* *therefore,* and *as a result* may be followed by an effect.

Some Europeans wanted to live in America, <u>so</u> they settled and set up colonies.

> **TIP** A cause happens before an effect. However, in a sentence, an effect is often written first, followed by its cause.

George Washington leads his troops into battle.

2 Look for Causes and Effects

Find what happened. That is the effect. Then find why it happened. That is the cause.

What happened? (effect)

People in the colonies became unhappy with British rulers.

Why did it happen? (cause)

<u>Because</u> they thought they were treated unfairly.

Read this history passage and think about the connection between cause and effect.

Why the Intolerable Acts Were Passed

Effect →

During the 1760s, people in the American colonies became angry because of some British laws that were passed. Some

Cause → laws placed taxes on British goods sold in the colonies, so the colonists bought fewer

Effect → British goods. The colonists disliked the tax on imported British tea. Since they did not like the tax, some colonists took all the tea from a British ship and dumped it into Boston Harbor.

Cause This event became known as "The Boston Tea Party." The laws called the Intolerable Acts were passed because the British wanted to punish the colonists for the Boston Tea Party.

Effect

Determine Cause and Effect

Read the paragraph below. Find at least four examples of cause and effect relationships.

The First Continental Congress

A group of American colonists met on September 5, 1774, because they were unhappy with British control of the colonies. They called their meeting the First Continental Congress. British leaders had passed some laws that the colonists called the Intolerable Acts. One law closed the Port of Boston, so ships could not enter or leave with things to sell. Another law ordered the colonists to allow British troops to stay in their homes. At the meeting, the colonists wrote a letter asking King George of Britain to change his laws, because they thought the laws were unfair. The laws were not changed, so the colonists became even angrier. Because the colonists did not want to be ruled by Britain, the Revolutionary War soon began.

TEST TIP

On some tests you may need to find causes and effects in a reading passage. When you come to a cause and effect question, go back and find cue words in the reading passage.

Skill 14

HOW TO

Tell Fact from Opinion

The Pony Express

Clinging to the backs of galloping horses, Pony Express riders risked their lives to carry messages across the country. When you read about events in history such as the Pony Express, you learn facts about people, places, and events. A **fact** is a true statement. It can be proved or checked. Names, dates, places, and events are facts. Learning how to find the facts in a reading can help you understand events in history.

Before the U.S. Postal Service was founded, mail delivery took weeks or even months. Letters would have to be carried on slow-moving wagons or boats, and even important messages could not be sent quickly over long distances. The Pony Express was started to solve these problems. Mail carriers raced between stations along the 2,000 mile route between East and West, changing horses every 25 miles. With riders traveling about 200 miles per day at top speed, letters could be delivered in ten days. Although ten days seems like a long time, the Pony Express was considered rush delivery in the year 1860.

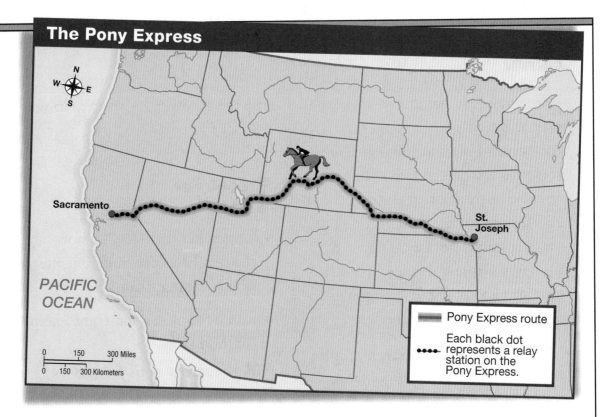

The Pony Express

Sacramento

PACIFIC OCEAN

St. Joseph

0   150   300 Miles
0   150   300 Kilometers

Pony Express route

Each black dot represents a relay station on the Pony Express.

Look for facts in the following paragraph about the Pony Express.

In 1860 and 1861, the Pony Express delivered mail. Riders on horseback carried letters between Saint Joseph, Missouri, and Sacramento, California. The two cities are about 2,000 miles apart. Each mail carrier rode for almost 200 miles a day. Riders changed horses every 25 miles at relay stations. Some Pony Express riders, such as Bill Cody and Johnny Fry, became famous. Although it operated for only 19 months, the Pony Express is an important part of U.S. history.

TIP If you could do research to confirm the truth of a statement, it is a fact.

Fact: In 1860 and 1861, the Pony Express delivered mail.

Fact: Riders carried mail between Saint Joseph, Missouri, and Sacramento, California.

69

STEPS IN Telling Fact from Opinion

When you read about history, you may also read people's opinions. An **opinion** is a statement of what someone believes or feels. Opinions are neither true nor false. You cannot check or prove an opinion. Look at these opinions from a customer of the Pony Express. Notice how the opinions about The Pony Express are different from the facts.

"Mail delivered by boat or wagon takes much too long to go from Saint Joseph to Sacramento. Even though it costs $5 for each letter, it is better to use the Pony Express. I think ten days is long enough to have to wait for mail. It seems like the riders are young and strong enough to ride more than 200 miles a day."

Opinion: "...it is better to use the Pony Express."

Opinion: "I think ten days is long enough to have to wait for mail."

Use the following steps to help you tell fact from opinion.

1 Look for Facts

- Remember that facts do not change. Facts are true no matter who is stating them.

- Names of places sometimes help you find facts.

Riders carried mail from Saint Joseph, Missouri, to Sacramento, California.

- Facts may be about people. Look for people's names to help find these facts.

Some Pony Express riders, such as Bill Cody and Johnny Fry, became famous.

- Make sure the statement can be checked or proved.

Riders changed horses at relay stations. Yes, it can be checked in an encyclopedia.

2 Look for Opinions

Remember that opinions cannot be proven true or false. Opinions are a person's feelings or beliefs.

Certain words give clues that a statement may be an opinion. Look for clue words such as *think, believe, good, better, best, wonderful, bad, worst, terrible, more, most, seems,* and *should.*

"It seems like the riders are young and strong enough to ride more than 200 miles a day."

"I think ten days is long enough to have to wait for mail."

3 Compare and Contrast Facts and Opinions

When you read, paragraphs may include both facts and opinions. It may help to list the facts and opinions in a chart.

Facts	Opinions
Most Pony Express riders were teenage boys.	The Pony Express should have hired only adult riders.
The riders changed horses every 25 miles.	I think a fast, 25-mile ride is too hard on a horse.
The Pony Express ended after 19 months.	It is too bad the Pony Express ended so soon.

Imagine a Pony Express rider wrote the diary entry below. He might write about what he did and felt on his rides. Think about facts and opinions as you read the entry.

September 10, 1860

I work hard and take many risks to deliver the mail. For such a dangerous job, I should be paid more. Today, the trail was hot and dusty. The ground was rough and full of holes. Several times, my horse nearly stumbled. By the time I reached the third changing station, my horse was sweating and breathing very hard. I think 25 miles was too far for him to run at high speed. It would be better to put changing stations closer together.

Opinion

Fact →

Opinion

Pony Express rider approaching relay station

Tell Fact from Opinion

Read the paragraph below. Find one fact and one opinion.

The Short Life of the Pony Express

The Pony Express began delivering mail in April, 1860. Its owners charged five dollars to deliver each letter. They should have made money, but instead the owners of the Pony Express lost money. By late 1861, a new railroad and a telegraph system had been built across the country. Messages could be sent much faster by train or telegraph, so the Pony Express was no longer needed. Still, it was wrong to take jobs away from the riders.

TEST TIP

On some tests you need to tell whether a statement is a fact or an opinion. As you read each statement, ask yourself if you could prove it true or false. A fact can be checked. If a statement cannot be proven true or false, then it is an opinion.

Skill 15
HOW TO
Draw Conclusions

Amelia Earhart, 1931

Amelia Earhart's Mysterious Disappearance

Amelia Earhart was a famous airplane pilot. In the 1930s, when she became the first woman to fly across the Atlantic Ocean alone, very few pilots were women. Earhart was an inspiration to women that they, too, could follow their dreams. The world watched Earhart's amazing flying career as she set one world record after another. Then, in 1937, Amelia Earhart suddenly disappeared while flying over the Pacific Ocean. To this day, no one knows what happened to her.

Historians sometimes try to solve mysteries from the past by looking at facts. Facts that give information about an event are called **evidence.** If you gather enough evidence about something, you can draw a **conclusion** about what happened. When you draw a conclusion, you are making a decision. You use evidence like pieces of a puzzle, putting them together until you have a picture of what could have happened. Then you decide what your conclusion will be.

For example, suppose a plane lands carrying only one person. At least one person is needed to fly a plane. A woman gets out of the plane. From this evidence, you can draw the conclusion that the woman is the pilot, because she had to be the one who flew the plane.

Use these steps to help you draw conclusions.

1 Find the Facts

Suppose you need to draw a conclusion about an event in history. What facts are known about the event? Find as many details as you can.

Pilot Amelia Earhart made several long flights. Her last flight was in 1937.

Jet airplanes were not yet in use during the 1930s.

2 Examine and Organize Evidence

Make sure that you include only important information in your collection of evidence. How do the facts fit together? Do you have enough evidence collected to draw a conclusion about your event?

EVIDENCE

The woman got out of the plane after it landed. She was the only person on the plane.

CONCLUSION

The woman was the pilot of the plane.

3 Use the Evidence to Draw a Conclusion

Use your evidence to make a decision about your topic event. For example, Earhart stopped flying before jet planes were in use. Therefore, you can conclude that she did not fly jets. Suppose you also know that planes without jet engines have propellors. Then you can conclude that Earhart flew planes with propellors.

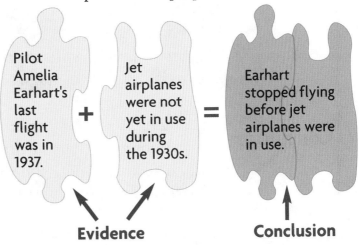

Pilot Amelia Earhart's last flight was in 1937. + Jet airplanes were not yet in use during the 1930s. = Earhart stopped flying before jet airplanes were in use.

Evidence   **Conclusion**

Read this history passage. Think about the conclusion the writer has drawn and the evidence that supports it.

∽ Amelia Earhart ∽

In 1928, Amelia Earhart became the first woman to fly across the Atlantic Ocean as a passenger. Later, in 1932, Earhart was the first woman to fly across the Atlantic Ocean alone. She made the flight in about 15 hours. No one had ever made the flight in such a short time. The flight earned her awards from both the U.S. government and the French government.

In the year 1935, Earhart became the first woman to fly over the Pacific Ocean between Hawaii and California. That same year, she set another record. She flew nonstop from Mexico City to New York City in 14 hours and 19 minutes, the fastest trip ever made between those two cities.

Earhart worked hard for the rights of women. Her achievements gave other women hope and encouragement. Besides being a woman pilot, she was one of the fastest pilots in the world.

Evidence

Evidence

Conclusion

Draw a Conclusion

Use evidence from the paragraph to draw a conclusion about what could have happened to Amelia Earhart.

Amelia Earhart's Last Flight

In June 1937, Amelia Earhart set out to fly around the world. Navigator Frederick Noonan went with her. His job was to give her information so she could fly in the right direction. They began in Miami, Florida, and flew east. Using a two-way radio, Earhart made reports, telling people where they were. The last time anyone heard from them was on July 2, 1937. In Earhart's last radio transmissions, she gave the plane's location and said that fuel was running low. Planes and ships from the U.S. Navy searched for the missing fliers for more than two weeks. Searchers could not find Earhart, Noonan, or the plane. No trace of them has ever been found.

TEST TIP On some tests you may need to choose the correct conclusion based on facts in a reading passage. Read all the answer choices and choose the answer that is supported by all the facts.

Skill 16
HOW TO
Make a Decision

Volunteers Wanted

Volunteers are people who give their time and skills to help others. If you were interested in doing volunteer work, you would have to make a decision about what kind of work you would like to do.

A **decision** is a choice you make. You make decisions every day. You decide what to wear, what to eat, or when to do homework. Decisions like these are usually easy to make.

Dog walkers wanted. Call the Humane Society for more information. 991–0000.

Some decisions are more difficult. We all face choices about how to spend our time, money, and energy. Our choices can even affect the whole community. For example, you could choose to give to your community through volunteer work. Some volunteers visit elderly people, prepare food for the hungry, care for animals, or keep public areas clean. Volunteers are not paid, but most volunteers really enjoy helping others. How could you decide what kind of volunteer work would be best for you?

The following steps can help you make a decision.

1 Set Goals

What do you want to accomplish? Think about what is most important to you. Make a list of the goals you want to achieve.

My Goals as a Volunteer:

Help my community
Work with people
Get there by myself
Have fun

2 Identify Choices

Think about what you have to choose. Are you deciding what you want to do, buy, or make? Are you deciding where to go or how to spend your time? Think about the possibilities. Find and list as many choices as you can.

3 Consider Choices

What are the advantages and disadvantages of each choice? These may be facts or your own feelings about the choices. Make a list or chart to help you organize and consider your choices.

4 Make Your Decision

Think about which choice will help you achieve your goals. How does each choice affect other people? After thinking about the advantages and disadvantages, make a careful decision. Try out your choice.

5 Evaluate Your Decision

Does your choice help you meet your goals? Does it feel right to you? If not, you might want to rethink your choice. You may wish to change your decision.

Read the chart below. See how one student used the chart to identify choices, compare choices, and make a decision about volunteering.

VOLUNTEER OPTIONS

Place	Kind of Work	Advantages	Disadvantages
School	Tutoring	I like little kids. It would be easy to get there. Maybe I could get Nia to volunteer with me!	I would spend a long day at school.
Library	Shelving books	It would be easy to get there.	Working alone is boring.
Humane Society	Dog-walking	I LOVE dogs! Mom likes dogs, too.	Someone would have to drive me there. They require adult supervision.
Health Care Center	Visiting with senior citizens	I would be with people. Close to home—I could walk there.	Have to wear a uniform.

List helps organize choices

Feeling

Fact

A decision

Making a Decision

Read about the volunteer jobs below. Make a list or chart to help you decide which one would be best for you.

Cat Rescue Center— Helpers needed to care for cats and kittens. Feed, clean cages, and play with cats. Adult supervision required.

Volunteers Wanted! Adopt a grandparent! Visit, help with chores, and be a friend. One visit per week, any day.

Local park seeks volunteers to help collect litter from nature trails. Two hours per week. Permission from parent required.

Be a playground pal! Help keep kids safe on the playground. An adult works with you. Saturday mornings at the city playground.

Help with story hour. Read to four-year-olds. School day care center. Tuesdays after school.

TEST TIP

You make a decision every time you choose an answer on a test. Read all the choices before you decide. Decide which ones are clearly wrong. Then pick your answer from the remaining choices.

HOW TO

Take Notes

The Colonies Break Free

All men are created equal and have rights! The King of Great Britain has trampled the rights of the American colonists! The people of America demand self-government! Therefore, the colonies are declaring their freedom from British rule!

This paragraph tells what the American colonists wanted to say to Great Britain. The message was written to the British king, George III, in a long document called the Declaration of Independence. In 1776, men from each of the thirteen American colonies came together to sign the declaration at the Second Continental Congress.

The Declaration of Independence became one of the most important documents in U.S. history.

To learn more about the Declaration of Independence, you could read and do research about it. To help yourself remember details from your reading and research, you could take notes. **Taking notes** is writing down important facts, ideas, and opinions about a topic while reading or listening. Note taking is a very valuable and important skill.

You can learn how to take notes by following the steps on the next three pages.

1 Collect Information

Find answers to the questions Who, What, When, Where, Why, and How. Look for answers to any other questions you can think to ask about your subject. Questions will help you choose sources, look for information, and decide which facts are important.

To find information, use sources such as history books, encyclopedias, biographical dictionaries, newspapers, magazines, documentary videos, and interviews.

Members of the Second Continental Congress signing the Declaration of Independence

2 Organize Your Information

You can organize your information in many ways. Here are a few ideas.

Make a Gathering Grid.

A **gathering grid** is a simple chart that you can use to sort information. To make a gathering grid, draw a grid like the one below. Write your topic and leave a space for your sources across the top. Write your questions in the left column, and your answers in the columns to the right. You may need to add columns as you add more sources and find more facts.

Thomas Jefferson

John Adams

Benjamin Franklin

GATHERING GRID		
Declaration of Independence:	*Encyclopedia*	*History Book*
When was it signed?	July 4, 1776	After 2nd Continental Congress met
Who wrote it?	Thomas Jefferson	John Adams and Benjamin Franklin helped

Use Index Cards.

Index cards are a great way to keep and organize notes. Write one note on each index card, and arrange them in any order you like. You can quickly flip through the index cards to find the notes you need.

Write Subject Headings.

Subject headings are like titles that explain what a passage is about. For example, if you are looking in an encyclopedia for information about John Adams, you would search alphabetically for the subject heading, "Adams, John." Write subject headings on your note paper or index cards. Then record your notes under the correct headings.

3 Write the Information

When reading, listening, watching, or even thinking, take clear notes that you can read and understand later. Use your own words when writing notes. Make your notes short. You do not need to write notes in complete sentences. Use key words, phrases, and abbreviations. Summarize the most important information.

2nd Continental Congress tells T. Jefferson to write Dec. of Ind.

Note where you found the information. Include the title of the source, author, date of publication, and page number.

"Declaration of Independence." Britannica Junior. 1961. 5: 41.

A **quote** is exact words that someone has said. If you copy a quote in your notes, make sure to use quotation marks. Also make careful notes of who said each and every quote you use.

"Well, if you are decided, I will do as well as I can," said Thomas Jefferson when he was asked to write the Declaration of Independence.

TIP If you use an author's exact words, put them in quotation marks.

EXAMPLE OF Taking Notes

Study the sample notes below.

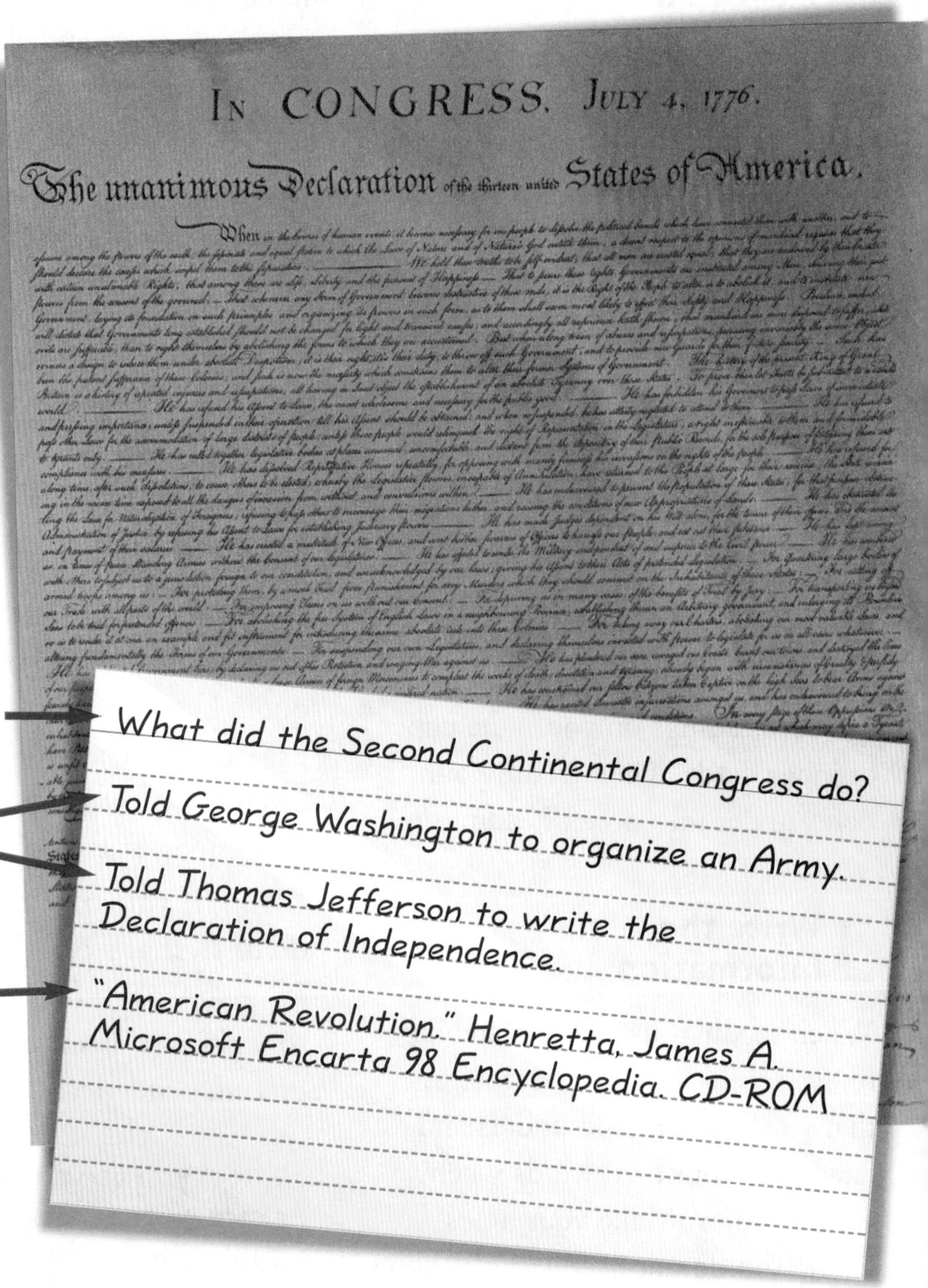

IN CONGRESS, JULY 4, 1776.
The unanimous Declaration of the thirteen united States of America.
What did the Second Continental Congress do?
Told George Washington to organize an Army.
Told Thomas Jefferson to write the Declaration of Independence.
"American Revolution." Henretta, James A.
Microsoft Encarta 98 Encyclopedia. CD-ROM

Start with questions

Write notes in few words

Write the source

Take Notes

Take notes on the article below.

Writing the Declaration of Independence

The Second Continental Congress was a meeting of representatives from all thirteen American colonies. When it met in 1775, fighting with the British had begun. Shots had been fired, but the colonists had not discussed a common purpose for the fighting.

At the Second Continental Congress, the representatives decided the colonies should be free of British rule. They also decided that they should tell the British king and the world in writing that they were independent.

Thomas Jefferson wrote the Declaration of Independence. It listed complaints about Great Britain and said the colonies were free. The Declaration of Independence was signed by members of the Continental Congress on July 4, 1776.

TEST TIP

On some tests you may need to choose the best example of notes about a written passage. Read all the answer choices. Choose the one that gives all the important information in very few words.

HOW TO

Recognize a Point of View

Gettysburg: Two Points of View

The American Civil War broke out when the Southern, or Confederate, states decided they did not want to be part of the United States. The Northern, or Union, states fought the Confederate states to keep them all under one government. One of the most famous battles of the Civil War took place in Gettysburg, Pennsylvania, in July of 1863. It is known as the Battle of Gettysburg.

A description of a historical event may be written by a person who took part in the event. A writer who was involved in an event will tell about it from his or her own **point of view** —a personal way of looking at the world around them.

Different writers often have very different points of view, or personal feelings and opinions, about the same event. For example, one description of the Battle of Gettysburg could be written from the point of view of a Confederate soldier. If another description was written from a Union soldier's point of view, it would probably be very different. Writers' personal experiences affect the way they feel about what happened.

Below is an example of a Confederate soldier's point of view.

I was 20 when the Civil War began. The Union wanted to keep us in the United States. But in Georgia and other southern states, we wanted to be independent and live by our own laws. I was proud to defend our way of life in the South by serving in the Confederate army.

STEPS IN Recognizing a Point of View

1 Find Clue Words

Words such as *I, me, we, us, my,* and *our* tell you that the writer was present at the event. These clue words can be used to help you figure out the writer's point of view. For example, how could you tell if a Union soldier or a Confederate soldier wrote the following passage?

General George Meade of the Union Army

General Robert E. Lee of the Confederate Army

General Meade was my commander. As leader of the Union Army, General Meade proved his strength.

By finding the clue word <u>my</u>, you can tell that the writer was with the same army as General Meade. Because of information given about General Meade, you can tell that the writer was a Union soldier.

2 Look for Feelings and Opinions

Look for words describing thoughts, opinions, and feelings. When a writer tells about his or her own feelings, you find out how he or she views an event. Having a clear understanding of a writer's feelings and opinions is a good way to recognize a personal point of view.

General Robert E. Lee was the great leader of the Confederate Army. I was <u>proud</u> to fight under a hero such as General Lee.

This passage tells you that the writer was proud to be on the same side of a battle as General Lee. Because of information given about General Lee, you can tell that the writer was a Confederate soldier.

89

Read the following historical passage written by a Confederate soldier. Focus on the writer's thoughts and feelings about the battle of Gettysburg.

Battle of Gettysburg — Clue word

Clue word →

Feeling →

Clue word

Clue word →

Feeling →

Opinion →

> Today, July 3, we met the Union army at Gettysburg. At General Lee's order, we charged them from across the field. At first I was not afraid. Then the Union soldiers fired, and my friends and neighbors began falling before my eyes. I heard gunfire, cannon blasts, and the screaming of the wounded. I was more frightened than I had ever been in my life. We had to run for our lives, away from the Union army. That day, about 28,000 brave men were killed fighting for their independence.

Recognize a Point of View

Read the passage below about the Battle of Gettysburg. Find the writer's point of view.

The Battle of Gettysburg

I felt proud to defend Gettysburg against the attack by Confederate troops. As I remember, fighting began on July first. As the enemy attacked, we were forced to fall back. I think General Meade was planning ahead when he ordered us to retreat that first day. On July third, events turned in our favor. Thousands of Confederate soldiers faced us across a field. Suddenly they began to charge.

Our soldiers started firing as fast as they could. We forced the Confederates to turn and run. We had won the battle, but at heart-breaking cost. Thousands of brave Union soldiers were killed or wounded. Although our Union Army suffered great losses at the Battle of Gettysburg, we were rewarded with victory over Lee's army.

TEST TIP

On some tests you may need to identify a point of view in a reading passage. If the passage contains the writer's own thoughts, feelings, or opinions, it is written from that writer's personal point of view.

Skill 19

Understand an Advertisement

Who Says It's Good?

Every day you see many advertisements, or ads, for products. Ads are on TV, in magazines and newspapers, and on billboards. An **advertisement** is a way to get information about a product. With catchy advertising, the maker of the product tries to get you to buy it.

One way to convince you to buy is through endorsements. An **endorsement** is the use of a famous person to help sell a product. Look at the ad on this page. It has an endorsement. Would the product look as good to you without the athlete's endorsement of it? Does this ad make you want to buy the product? Think about different ads you have seen that use a famous person to endorse a product.

The steps on the next page will help you understand these ads.

STAR ATHLETIC SHOES

MORE POWERFUL THAN EVER!

"Use them and you will run like a champion!" says Mark Johnson, three-time winner of the National Running Championship.

Available in all sizes and widths

Endorsement

1 Look for Helpful Information

Facts and truthful details are helpful information. The ad for Star Athletic Shoes says that all sizes and widths are available. This is useful information for shoe buyers.

2 Look for Loaded Words

Loaded words are words that try to persuade you but don't give facts. In the ad for Star Athletic Shoes, loaded words are *"More powerful than ever!"* In what way are the shoes more powerful than ever? The ad doesn't give you any facts that support this claim.

3 Examine the Images

Besides words, ads often contain images to persuade you to buy the product. Look at the Star ad. The champion runner is shown wearing his Star Athletic Shoes. The picture

TIP **Keep in mind when you see a product endorsement that people are usually paid for giving endorsements.**

suggests that if you buy the shoes, you will win races. There is no proof, however, that buying the product will make you a champion runner.

4 Judge the Claims Made

Look at any endorsement in an ad, and ask yourself these questions. *Who* says it's good? Does this person have the *experience* to judge if the product is good? Could that product be the *only* reason for the person's success? In the Star ad, Mark Johnson is a champion athlete, so maybe the athletic shoes are good. However, Mark also trained very hard. So you can not be sure the shoes are the *only* reason for his success.

How to Understand an Advertisement

Read the following ad for Bright Toothpaste. Notice how the ad uses words and pictures to persuade you to buy the product.

Loaded words

For that guaranteed white, bright smile!

Endorsed by National Running Champion Mark Johnson

Endorsement

BRIGHT TOOTHPASTE

Helpful Words

Now in two flavors – orange and peppermint

USE THIS SKILL

Understand an Advertisement

Read the following ad about a sports drink. Then answer the questions below.

1. What are the helpful words or facts?

2. What are the loaded words?

3. How does the picture make you feel about the product?

4. Is the endorsement a reason to buy the product? Why or why not?

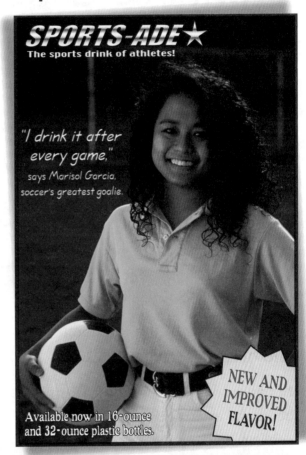

SPORTS-ADE ★
The sports drink of athletes!

"I drink it after every game," says Marisol Garcia, soccer's greatest goalie.

NEW AND IMPROVED FLAVOR!

Available now in 16-ounce and 32-ounce plastic bottles.

TEST TIP

Some tests may ask you to show that you understand an advertisement. Before you answer any questions, look carefully at the words in the ad. Decide if the ad contains facts or opinions. Opinions in ads often use loaded words that give false information.

Skill 20

HOW TO

Work in a Group

Making a Group Decision

Often in school you will need to work together with your classmates on a group project. When you **work in a group,** you have to help each other achieve a goal. You will have to make choices and decisions as a group.

Students bartering at a school trade fair

Suppose your group goal is to learn about the exchange of goods and services by bartering at a class trade fair. To **barter** means to trade or exchange goods or services without using money. There are many ways to barter. For example, people barter goods, such as food or clothing, for other goods. People also barter services, such as repairing a car or cutting someone's hair, for other services. Goods can be bartered for services, and services can be bartered for goods. Your group will have to decide both what to barter and how to barter.

Learn how to make decisions and work in a group by following the steps on the next page.

Group Plan

Goal

A. Our project is: _____

B. Things we need to do: _____
Tasks

Jobs for everyone

C. Jobs for each group member: _____
Name: _____ Job: _____

D. Schedule: ◄——— **Schedule**
Job: _____ Date Due: _____

1 Make a Group Plan

Your group should first talk about your project. What exactly is your assignment? Does everyone understand the goal? As you talk, each person should have a chance to share his or her ideas. It is very important that members of your group listen carefully when a group member is talking. You should try to reach a decision that everyone in the group agrees with. When you have a group decision about your goal, write it down.

TIP Take notes on everyone's ideas. Then combine the best parts of everyone's ideas into a plan on which everyone agrees.

2 Figure Out Tasks

Once you are clear about your goal, your group should decide what needs to be done to achieve it. Each group member must choose a task or job to do. The work should be divided as evenly as possible.

3 Keep to a Schedule

Group members should agree when they will have each task finished. Write down a schedule for when each task will be completed.

Read the following group plan for a class project on bartering.

	Goal	**Group Plan**

Goal →

Our project goal: Learn how to barter goods for other goods. When you barter, you don't use money. Instead, you trade things of equal value. You find somebody who wants what you have and has something you want. Then you trade. We have decided that

Tasks → our group will make and barter bookmarks for other items at the class fair.

A. **Things we need to do:**

- Get paper for bookmarks

Jobs for • Cut paper into strips

everyone • Decorate strips with a stencil, stickers, yarn, glue, and glitter

    • Clean up mess

B. **Jobs for each group member:**

Name: Michelle	Job: get paper
Name: LaToya	Job: cut paper
Name: Michelle	Job: decorate strips
Ian	
LaToya	
Name: Ian	Job: clean up

Schedule →

C. **Schedule:**

Job: get paper	Date Due: October 15
Job: cut paper	Date Due: October 18
Job: decorate strips	Date Due: October 24
Job: clean up	Date Due: October 24

Final Project Due Date: October 26

USE THIS SKILL

Work in a Group

Work with classmates to create a group plan for making something to barter at a class trade fair. Look over the pictures below of objects you might make. You may wish to use the headings and lines below to record your group plan.

Group Plan

A. Our project is: _____

B. Things we need to do: _____

C. Jobs for each group member:

   Name:_____ Job: _____

D. Schedule: _____

Job:_____ Date Due: _____

Writing and Research Skills

Skill 21

Write a Paragraph

Jane Addams: A Good Neighbor

In the 1800s and early 1900s, life in American cities was hard for many new citizens. Many families arrived in the United States with little more than the clothes on their backs. Cities were crowded with people, and living conditions were horrible in some places. Entire neighborhoods were in desperate need of jobs, medical care, clothing, food, education, and more. Thanks to the kindness of people like Jane Addams, there was hope for a better life for the poor.

The sentences above are grouped in a paragraph. A **paragraph** is a group of two or more sentences that tells about one main idea. Many

Jane Addams, the "Mother of Social Work"

writings are divided into paragraphs to clearly separate ideas from one another. A **topic sentence** introduces the main idea of a paragraph. The other sentences in the paragraph give information to support the main idea.

You can learn how to write a paragraph by following the steps on the next page.

STEPS IN Writing a Paragraph

1 Write a Topic Sentence

First decide what you are going to write about. Are you writing a story, a report for school, or a letter? Gather any information you may need. Then write a topic sentence to begin your paragraph. The topic sentence should tell your reader what the paragraph is about.

2 Write Supporting Sentences

Write sentences to support the main idea. These should give details, reasons, and examples of what the topic sentence tells the reader. For example, this supporting sentence tells why life was hard for some immigrants:

Entire neighborhoods were in desperate need of jobs, medical care, clothing, food, education, and more.

Every sentence in a paragraph should give information to support the main idea. A **closing sentence** at the end of your paragraph should complete the main idea:

Thanks to the kindness of people like Jane Addams, there was hope for a better life for the poor.

3 Revise and Edit Your Paragraph

Read your paragraph. Does your topic sentence state the main idea? Do all the other sentences support the main idea? If not, cross out words that do not belong. Do you have enough details to support the main idea? If not, add more information. To **revise** is to make these kinds of changes. When you have made the other changes, **edit** your work by correcting errors in spelling, grammar, and punctuation. Write or type a neat final copy of your paragraph.

Read the following paragraph. Notice the topic sentence, supporting sentences, and closing sentence.

Jane Addams Opens Hull House

Topic sentence

Hull House in Chicago was America's first "settlement house," or community aid center. Jane Addams opened Hull House because she wanted to help the poor. The Hull House staff started helping people find jobs. It offered classes in English for people new to America. Addams and her friends helped immigrants adapt to life in the United States. The staff at Hull House also helped set up libraries, playgrounds, and camps for children. Soon other community aid centers opened all over the country. Settlement houses like Hull House were sources of help and hope for many Americans.

Supporting sentences

Closing sentence

Write a Paragraph

Research and write a paragraph about one of the following topics.

- Jane Addams worked for peace during and after World War I.
- Jane Addams was president of the Women's International League for Peace and Freedom from 1915–1929.
- Jane Addams became chairperson of the Women's Peace Party in 1915.
- For her peace work, Jane Addams was awarded and shared the Nobel Peace Prize with an American educator in 1931.

TEST TIP

On some tests you may need to write a paragraph. Your paragraph should begin with a topic sentence. All the ideas in the paragraph should support the topic sentence.

HOW TO

Write a Description

Chinese Workers Come to America

The thin, stooped man swung his hammer high in the air, bringing it down with a loud *clang!* upon the steel railroad spike. His tan skin was wrinkled and burned by the sun, his hands blistered and bandaged with tattered gray rags. His dirt-smeared forehead glistened in the hot California sun as he struck the spike again and again. The frantic buzzing of locusts and the sharp clatter of hundreds of hammers rang in his ears as he worked. He thought again of his family far away in China. He hoped the money he earned on the railroad would be enough to help them.

Between the years 1849 and 1879, thousands of Chinese people sailed to America to find work. Times were hard in China, and people had heard about jobs on the railroad and in the California gold fields. By the year 1879, there were almost 75,000 Chinese people living and working in California.

Someone telling about a railroad worker from China could write a description about him. A **description** is a way to make a picture with words. Descriptions help readers imagine the things, places, people, actions or events in your writing. Descriptions can tell about a writer's thoughts, feelings, or experiences.

Follow the steps to learn how to write a description.

1 Decide on a Topic

Decide exactly what you want to describe. To get ideas, ask yourself some of these questions and list the answers.

Who? — *A Chinese man*

What? — *Working on the railroad*

When? — *In the 1860s*

Where? — *In California*

Why? — *To earn money*

2 Include Details

What people or objects are part of the scene? What details will help your readers picture them? Use descriptive words and verbs to paint a picture of your topic.

The golden dawn sunshine burst forth from behind the icy mountaintops. The muffled snaps of twigs sounded from beneath the workers' boots as they crunched along the forest path.

3 Use Words about the Five Senses

Describe what a person would see, hear, feel, smell, and taste.

Jian Li heard the high shriek of the whistle that signaled the end of the work day. He dropped his pick with a thud on the dry, dusty ground. He took a small orange from his pocket. Sinking his teeth into the bitter skin, he felt the orange's sweet, sticky juice wash over his dry mouth.

bright smooth sharp
heavy dusty
sour yellow
soft

TIP It sometimes helps to brainstorm ideas for descriptive words and verbs before you begin writing.

This description might have been written by a passenger on the Transcontinental Railroad, which was completed in 1869. Notice the details about senses and the descriptive words. Look for the verbs used in each sentence.

Descriptive

The spring sun warmed my face as the huge, black train engine drew near. A long, deep whistle broke the morning silence, and a whiff of hot burning coal floated on the light breeze. As the sturdy brake man put on the brakes, the smell of the heated iron tracks and wheels hit my nose. The train slowed to a stop, and a loud hiss exploded from the engine.

A month ago people couldn't have taken a fast train across this enormous country. More than 12,000 Chinese American workers had just finished laying the tracks. Over the cold winter they had worked long hours, the icy chill biting into their skin. Their tired muscles ached from stooping and lifting. Without their hard work, the Transcontinental Railroad would not have been finished so quickly. The other passengers and I had the workers to thank for this comfortable, fast way to travel.

Descriptive

USE THIS SKILL

Write a Description

Write a description in paragraph form. You can write about something you have seen or done, or you can pick one of the topics below. Read about your topic, do some research, and then write your description.

1. Chinese Americans working in the gold fields after the 1849 discovery of gold in California.

2. Chinese American workers building the Transcontinental Railroad that opened in 1869.

3. Chinatown in San Francisco during the late 1800s.

TEST TIP

Some tests may ask you to write a description. Think about what you are describing in your mind. What do you see, hear, feel, taste, or smell? Use descriptive words and verbs to express these ideas to the reader.

HOW TO

Write a Comparison/Contrast

What Was It Like to Live in 1900?

Have you ever wondered what life was like for young people in the past? Life in the year 1900 was very different than it is today. To better understand what it was like, you could compare and contrast the life of a child in 1900 to your own life.

One way that history writers can help their readers better understand the past is by doing comparison/contrast writing. When learning about two or more new ideas, people, and events, you might find it helpful to compare them to one another. A **comparison** describes ways that topic areas are the same. A **contrast** describes ways that topic areas are different.

Follow these steps to write a comparison/contrast.

1 Decide on Your Topic Areas

Before you begin writing, you should decide what people, places, things, or events you would like to compare and contrast. You may wish to write about two or three different topic areas.

2 Gather and Sort Information

Collect as much information as you can about each of your topic areas. Decide how your topics are alike and how they are different. Create a chart or Venn diagram to sort your information into "same" and "different" categories.

3 Use Adjectives and Signal Words

Begin writing about your topics, keeping a focus on comparing and contrasting them as you write. Words such as *taller* or *smaller* compare two subjects. Words such as *tallest* or *smallest* compare three or more subjects.

- Signal words such as **same, similar, like, both, as, also,** and **too** can tell how topic areas are similar. Words such as **unlike, but, more, less, than, better, worse,** and **different** show how things are different.

- Adjectives used to compare and contrast can end in *-er,* or *-est.*

Children in 1900 usually worked harder than children do today.

The largest libraries were in the cities.

- Adjectives used to contrast sometimes use the word *more.*

Usually life was more difficult for poor children than for children from wealthy families.

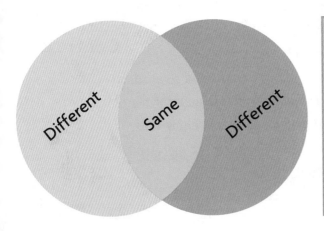

TIP Making a Venn diagram is an easy way to organize details as you prepare to write. Draw two large, overlapping circles. Write distinguishing details about each topic in the outer part of each circle. List things that are the same about both topics in the middle.

Read the following passage and think about how life in 1900 is compared and contrasted to life today.

Comparing and Contrasting Ways of Life

Compares

Around the year 1900, many children lived on farms. They lived in houses surrounded by trees and fields of crops. Like children today, they spent much of their time outdoors in the fresh air. Children worked beside their parents planting, weeding, and picking crops. Some cared for animals, cooked meals, and cleaned house. They had much less free time than children have today.

Contrasts

In cities, families often lived crowded together in tiny, dark apartments without windows. City streets were noisy, dirty, and often dangerous. Instead of fresh air, children breathed smoke from coal fires and factory chimneys. Some of them saw little of their parents, who worked long hours in factories. Unlike most young people today, many children had to work to earn money for their families instead of going to school. Many worked in factories, sold newspapers, worked in shops, ran errands, or cooked and cleaned.

Contrasts

Compares

When they were not working, they played many of the same sports and games that young people enjoy today. Still, most children in the year 1900 worked more and played less than children do today.

Write a Comparison/Contrast

Pick a topic from the list below. Write one or two paragraphs comparing and contrasting your life and life in 1900.

- The neighborhood of a farm child in 1900
- The neighborhood of a city child in 1900
- The work of a farm child in 1900
- The work of a city child in 1900
- The way a child in 1900 spent his or her free time
- The home of a farm child in 1900
- The home of a city child in 1900

TEST TIP	On some tests you may need to write a comparison/contrast of two subjects. A comparison shows how things are the same. A contrast shows how things are different.

Skill 24

HOW TO

Write a Journal Entry

The Trail of Tears

Imagine you are a Cherokee child in the year 1838. White men have discovered gold on your tribe's land. You and your family have been told that you must leave your home. Soldiers are forcing your people off their land and marching them to "Indian Territory" 800 miles away. Your house and all of your things are destroyed. How would you feel?

The "Indian Removal Act" was passed by the U.S. Congress in 1830. This act allowed President Andrew Jackson to force Native American people off their land. Jackson wanted the land to be given to white settlers and mined for gold. He told U.S. soldiers to move all the Native Americans west to "Indian Territory" in Oklahoma. The land where they were sent was not good for growing crops. It was land that no one else wanted.

A Cherokee child whose family was forced from his or her home might write about the experience in a journal. A **journal** is a place for a person to write about daily events in his or her life. A **journal entry** may cover a day, part of a day, or an event lasting several days. Historians can learn important details about events in the past by reading journals written by people long ago.

Historical fiction is a realistic story set in the past. Historical fiction stories are often written about real people and events in history. The writer sometimes makes up characters, dialogue, thoughts, and feelings. Writers of historical fiction sometimes tell a story in the form of a fictional journal entry. Journal entries help writers make the historical events seem more personal and realistic.

This journal entry might have been written by a Cherokee child in 1838. Think about how it helps the reader understand the child's experience and feelings.

November 21, 1838

The white soldiers pushed my family onto a wagon. There was not enough room for all of us, and my father and uncle had to walk. My sister said, "We will never see these mountains or our homes again." As we left our world behind, we all waved goodbye. Through my tears, I saw our things being thrown out of our house and taken by other people. I did not understand why we had to leave. I did not know where we were going.

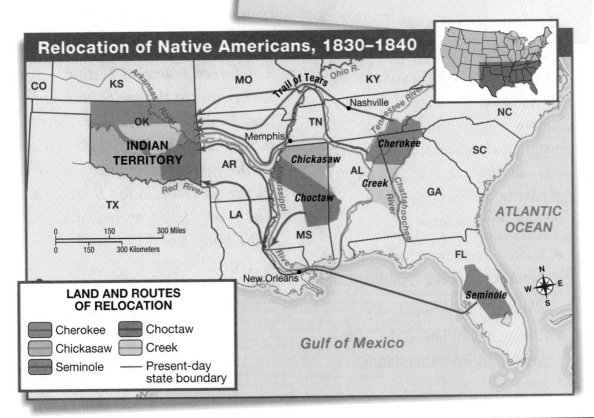

Relocation of Native Americans, 1830–1840

LAND AND ROUTES OF RELOCATION
- Cherokee
- Chickasaw
- Seminole
- Choctaw
- Creek
- Present-day state boundary

STEPS IN Writing a Journal Entry

1 Choose a Topic or Time Period

Decide what you would like to write about. You could write about the life of someone in the future or from the past. You might imagine you are an American living in the 1800s. For example, you could choose to write as a person affected by the Indian Removal Act of 1830.

2 Choose Your Writer

Decide what point of view you would like to show in your journal entry. You could imagine being a famous person in history or a historical character that you invent yourself. For example, you might choose to write as one of the following characters:

- Andrew Jackson, who ordered the removal of Native Americans from their lands.

- A soldier who forced the Native Americans from their lands.

- A settler who wanted the Native Americans' land.

- A Native American who was forced to go to Indian Territory.

3 List the Details

What information do you want to include? Think about the time, places, and people that you have chosen to write about. Use details from history to help readers understand your character's world.

The forced march of Native Americans to the west was a sad time in American history. Four thousand of the 15,000 Cherokees on the forced march died on the way from Georgia to Oklahoma. The route they traveled came to be known as "The Trail of Tears."

4 Think Like Your Character

Try to imagine the thoughts that your character might have had. Close your eyes and picture how living in their place and time would have been. Your reader should be able to see, hear, smell, taste, and feel that world through your words. Use thoughts and feelings to bring your character to life for the reader.

White families moved onto Cherokee lands in the 1830s.

Our first farm at last! I am so excited! We won one of the Indians' farms in the land lottery! I ran my fingers through the rich, dark earth, smelled the delicate wild roses, and walked through the canopy of trees in the forest. Father says we will cut down the trees to build a new house. I can't wait to help chop wood, plant the crops, and harvest.

I'm a little worried, though. I heard that the Cherokee are refusing to leave. My family needs this farmland. I hope there is no trouble when we move in.

Where you can, use some dialogue. Dialogue makes the events and characters seem more real and interesting. It can show the reader the thoughts and feelings of other characters involved in the incidents.

My daughter sobbed and screamed at a soldier in English, "No! Don't let them take our belongings!"

The soldier said roughly, "These aren't your belongings any more!"

TIP When using a direct quote, use quotation marks before and after what was said.

The following historical fiction is the journal entry of a soldier who removed Native Americans from their land. Notice the quotes, opinions, and feelings.

Feeling

A Day of Shame

For me this was a day of shame. I didn't become a soldier to drag helpless Indian men, women, and children from their homes. It took three soldiers to drag one strong man from his house. His little boy hung onto my leg sobbing and begging, "Please don't hurt my father!"

Thought

Quote

A woman begged to go back to her house for shoes and blankets. She held up a small girl and said, "Look. My poor daughter is barefoot. What will happen to her little feet?" The little girl was about my daughter's age. I felt so sorry for her.

Feeling

"Can't we let her get some shoes and blankets?" I asked the sergeant.
He looked at the ground and said, "We have orders not to let them back into their houses."

Quote

We pushed and dragged them to the wagons. It was so crowded that many had to walk. Some of the Indians were very old and they looked tired and sick. I was worried that the trip west would be hard for them.

Thought

Write a Journal Entry

Pick one of these real or fictional characters and write a journal entry from their point of view.

- President Jackson before or after ordering the removal of the Native Americans

- A white settler who received some Cherokee land from the U.S. government after the Indians were removed

- A soldier who removed the Cherokee and marched them on the "Trail of Tears"

- A Native American adult who was forced to move to Oklahoma

- A Native American child forced from the family home

TEST TIP On some tests you may need to write a journal entry for a character in fiction or a real person in history. Try to think like the character. Write in the way the character might have written.

Skill 25

HOW TO

Write a Business Letter

Solving a Problem

Have you ever had a problem with a product that you bought? Has the item broken easily, been missing a part, or not worked at all? One way to solve this kind of problem is to write a business letter. A **business letter** is a letter with a serious purpose.

Suppose you had a problem with a new bike helmet you had ordered. The chinstrap fell off after you had used it only a week. You could try to solve this problem by writing a letter of complaint to the manufacturer of the bike helmet. Writing a letter of complaint is an easy and effective way to inform a person or a business about a problem.

Follow the steps on the next page to write a business letter.

1 Plan Your Letter

Think about what your problem is and how you would like to solve it. Your problem should be something that the manufacturer—the company that made the product—can correct. Your solution should be something the manufacturer would probably want to do to keep you as a customer.

Next, find out to whom you should write. You may need to ask a teacher or family member for help in getting the right person and the correct address.

2 Draft Your Letter

Follow the business format shown on the next page.

Begin your letter by describing your problem in detail. Explain how you would like the problem to be solved. Keep your letter short so that a busy person can read it quickly. End by thanking the person for his or her help.

3 Revise and Edit

Proofread for spelling, capitalization, and punctuation. Make sure you have used correct grammar. Also check that your letter is in the correct business form shown on the next page. Have a teacher or family member check your work.

Five Parts of a Business Letter

1. The <u>heading</u> is your own address and the date.

2. The <u>inside address</u> is the address of the person to whom you are writing.

3. The <u>salutation</u> is a polite greeting, such as "Dear Mr." or "Dear Ms." followed by the last name of the person to whom you are writing.

4. The <u>body</u> is the main part of the letter, where you give information.

5. The <u>closing</u> is at the end of the letter, such as "Sincerely" or "Best regards" followed by your name and signature.

TIPS

➤ Do not use angry words in a business letter. Always be polite.

➤ If possible, use a computer to type your letter. Typewritten letters are easier to read.

4 Send Your Letter

Make a final neat copy of your letter to send. Always keep a copy of business letters you send in case you need to refer to them later.

EXAMPLE OF **Writing a Business Letter**

Study the sample business letter shown below.

739 Prince Street ← **Heading**
River Oaks, IA 43204

October 14, 2001

Mr. John Correlli, President ← **Inside address**
Correlli Bike Company
1390 Henderson Road
Big Town, CA 54321

Dear Mr. Correlli: ← **Salutation**

I ordered a Correlli Bike Safety Helmet from your catalogue three weeks ago. I have used the helmet for only a short time, but the chinstrap has broken already. My mother says the bolt holding it in place was defective, and it cannot be repaired. I would like to have a new helmet or my money back. I paid $16.59 for the helmet.

Thank you for your help in solving this problem. ← **Body**

Sincerely, ← **Closing**

Danielle Wu ← **Signature**
Danielle Wu

Write a Business Letter

Write a business letter to the following person about a flashlight you ordered that arrived broken. Use the illustration below to help you.

(Write your address here)
(Write the date here)

Ms. Eleanor Bower, President
Everyday Products
1650 Sunshine Avenue
Los Ricos, CA 60608

Dear _____:

Sincerely,
(Sign your name, then type or print your name below your signature.)

TEST TIP

Some tests may ask you to show correct punctuation marks on a business letter. Be sure to use a colon after the salutation. Use a comma to separate the day's date from the year, to separate cities and states, and after the closing.

Skill 26

HOW TO

Write a Summary

Hardships at Valley Forge

Many soldiers died in the American Revolutionary War, but they were not all killed in battle. Over the winter of 1777–1778, more than 2,000 soldiers died without seeing a single British soldier. They died from hunger, cold, and disease at the winter camp of Valley Forge.

The paragraph above gives a summary of what happened to soldiers at Valley Forge, without giving many details. A **summary** is a collection of main ideas about a topic. For example, you could

The Winter Camp at Valley Forge

explain the main ideas from an event during the Revolutionary War by writing a summary of what happened. Writing a summary can help you remember important ideas. It can help you review and remember a book, an article, a story, or a lesson.

The steps on the next two pages will help you write a summary.

1 Read Carefully

Read the selection that you would like to summarize. Look for main ideas that tell you what the selection is about. As you read, look for answers to questions such as Who, What, When, Where, Why, and How. Then carefully read the selection a second time. Take notes if you wish.

2 Plan Your Summary

Identify Topic Sentences.
A **topic sentence** introduces the main idea of a paragraph. The other sentences in the paragraph give details, reasons, and examples that support the main idea. For example:

The Battle of Saratoga

Americans had time to build up their forces while the British troops were on their way. *The British were traveling over rough ground. Their supply wagons moved slowly. Meanwhile, landowners and farmers came from all around and joined the American troops. By the time the British troops arrived, they were outnumbered.*

This topic sentence highlighted in blue gives the main idea of the paragraph.

The rest of the sentences give details.

If you identify and list all of the topic sentences in a reading, you will have some of the main ideas of a selection. Choose the main ideas that you want to include in your summary.

3 Write a First Draft

Organize your main ideas in the order you want them to appear in your summary. Use only important information. Begin writing your summary, including the most important idea in your first sentence. Write complete sentences.

General George Washington

4 Revise and Edit Your Draft

Read your first draft. Did you include the important ideas? If not, add them. Did you include any details that are not main ideas? If so, cross them out. Details should not be part of a summary. To **revise** is to make these kinds of changes. After you have made the other changes, **edit** your work by correcting errors in spelling, punctuation, and use of capital letters.

5 Publish Your Summary

Write a final draft, including all corrections. If you are using a computer, you can just make changes to your draft document before printing and saving your revision. If you are writing by hand, neatly copy your summary onto a clean sheet of paper.

> **TIP** Some readings have headings in boldface that tell you what the main ideas are. Sometimes the table of contents can help you find the main ideas in a book.

Read the following text about the life of Washington's troops at Valley Forge. Then read the example summary on the next page.

Washington's Winter Camp at Valley Forge

Topic sentences → General George Washington's army was forced to flee from Philadelphia. After the Revolutionary War broke out, British troops attacked Philadelphia, the home of the Continental Congress. The American army was outnumbered.

In December 1777, Washington and his army camped for the winter at Valley Forge, Pennsylvania. Washington chose Valley Forge for the winter because it was easy to defend. It was also close to York, Pennsylvania, where the Continental Congress was then meeting.

Topic sentences → Washington begged the Congress for food, but did not get enough supplies for his men. Many men at the camp froze or starved to death. Those who survived ate "Firecakes," a thin mixture of flour and water they heated over camp fires.

Of Washington's 10,000 men, more than 2,500 died at Valley Forge. Many of them were killed by disease. Others ran away, abandoning Washington's army.

Help finally arrived from Prussia and France. The French and Prussians sent some supplies and helped train and organize Washington's army.

Read the example summary below.

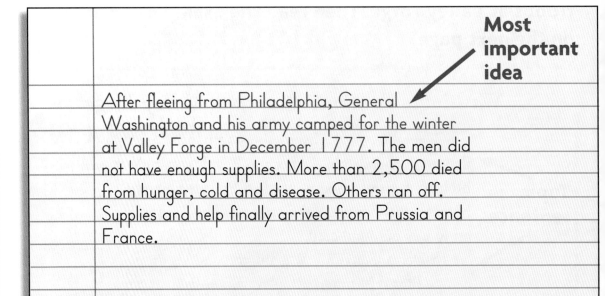

Most important idea

After fleeing from Philadelphia, General Washington and his army camped for the winter at Valley Forge in December 1777. The men did not have enough supplies. More than 2,500 died from hunger, cold and disease. Others ran off. Supplies and help finally arrived from Prussia and France.

Washington leads his army into battle.

Write a Summary

Write a summary of the following passage.

The Battle of Saratoga

The Battle of Saratoga was the turning point of the Revolutionary War. It took place because British general John Burgoyne wanted to capture the Hudson River Valley. He and his troops marched south from Canada into New York.

The British took a long time on the march. They were traveling over rough ground. Attacks from the American militia slowed them down.

The Americans had time to prepare and build up their forces. By the time the British troops arrived in Saratoga, New York, they were outnumbered by the Americans.

Eventually, the British troops had to surrender to the Americans at Saratoga. This was the first victory for the American Continental Army.

TEST TIP On some tests you may need to write short answers in your own words. Think about what you want to write, then write your thoughts clearly so other people can understand them.

Skill 27

HOW TO

Use the Internet

Who Are Your Representatives?

Did you know that there are people in Washington, D.C., making laws for you? Even if you aren't old enough to vote, they care what you think! You can use the Internet to find out who your representatives are.

The Senate and the House of Representatives make laws for the country. Two **senators** represent each state. Each state also has at least one **representative** in Congress. States with larger populations have more representatives. The people in each state elect senators and representatives. Together, the Senate and House of Representatives are called **Congress.**

You can use the Internet to find the names and addresses of your senators and congressional representatives. The **Internet** is a worldwide computer network. You can use the Internet as a valuable research tool.

To find the names of your senators and representatives, you will use a search engine. **Search engines** are programs that help you do word searches on the "Web," the World Wide Web. The **World Wide Web**

The U.S. Capitol

is a part of the Internet that allows you to easily connect to various Web sites. Who represents your state in Congress? You can find the answer on the Internet by following these steps.

TIP If a Web page gives good results, look at links on the page. The links may lead you to more good information. Links may be listed at the side of the page or at the bottom.

1 Choose a Search Engine

Your **Internet Service Provider** (ISP) is the company that connects your computer to the Internet. Your ISP may offer its own search engine. Ask your teacher to help you find a search engine to use.

2 Enter Keywords

Decide on the **keywords** for your search. These are main words related to the subject. For example, if you wanted to look up senators and representatives for the state of Ohio, you could enter the keywords "representatives" and "Ohio." Type your keywords into the search box and click on the search button.

3 Read Some Pages

The search engine will give you a list of Web pages based on your keywords. There could be three Web pages or three thousand! Look at some of the Web pages by clicking on their names.

4 Start Over

If you don't find what you want quickly, try a new search. This time, use different keywords or try another search engine. The Web has millions of pages. Keep searching for the ones you want!

Follow one student's journey through the Internet with a search engine. See how she found information about her congressional representative.

Jenna uses a search engine to search for "United States Congress." The screen shows ten entries—and says there are more than 100 pages that match her search!

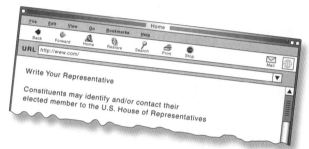

Jenna goes to the first page listed: "U.S. House of Representatives—107th Congress." Near the bottom of the page is a link called "Write Your Representative."

Jenna clicks on the blue words "Identify and/or contact." She follows directions on the next page and enters her state—Ohio—and her zip code—43214. She clicks the button to submit this information.

The next page shows her representative's name and gives her options to contact him. Because her representative's name is highlighted in blue, Jenna clicks on it to go to his Web page. There are 18 information links here! Now Jenna has all the information she needs.

Use the Internet

Use the Internet to find information about one of your state representatives and your two senators. Then answer the questions below.

1. What is the name of your state's congressional representative?

2. To what political party does your representative belong?

3. When was your representative first elected to Congress?

4. What are the names of your state's senators?

5. To what party does each of your senators belong?

6. When was each of your senators first elected to the U.S. Senate?

TEST TIP

Some tests may ask you to identify keywords for using a search engine on the Internet. Before answering questions about keywords, read the passage. Find the main words related to the subject. Some of these words should be correct keyword choices.

Skill 28

HOW TO

Use Reference Sources

Equality for ALL Men and Women

Imagine living in Alabama in 1955. African American students and white students had to go to different schools. African Americans could not use the same drinking fountains or rest rooms as white people. Some restaurants would not serve African Americans. They had to sit in different sections of buses, movie theaters, and other public venues. These unfair laws would not change until people got together and demanded their rights. It was time to put dreams of equality into action.

This unfair treatment of African Americans was allowed because of segregation. **Segregation** set people apart from one another because of their race. Although segregation was allowed by law, many people felt that it was wrong. People of every race, age, and religion began to work together to end unfair treatment of African Americans.

Dr. Martin Luther King, Jr., was a Baptist minister who worked to end segregation in the United States. He became one of the most famous leaders of the civil rights movement of the 1950s and 1960s. The **civil rights movement** was action taken by Americans who wanted to see African Americans receive equal opportunities and fair treatment. **Civil rights** are the rights that all U.S. citizens have, as written in the Constitution.

Dr. Martin Luther King, Jr., speaking at the March on Washington, August 1963.

Suppose you wanted to learn about segregation and the civil rights movement. You could look for information in reference sources. A **reference source** is a book or other source that gives facts about many different subjects. For example, you could look up *segregation* in an encyclopedia. **Encyclopedias** give general information about important people, topics, places, and events. They come in book form, online, or on CD-ROM, with topics arranged in alphabetical order. Encyclopedias often suggest additional books and other sources of information about your topic.

If you wanted to find out more about the life and work of Martin Luther King, Jr., you could look up his name in a *biographical dictionary*. A **biographical dictionary** lists important people alphabetically by last name. It gives a few facts about each person listed and tells why the person is important. In a biographical dictionary you could find out when Martin Luther King, Jr., was born, where he went to school, and why he is famous. Then if you wanted to learn more, you could check an encyclopedia. For even more information about Dr. King or other famous people, explore the biography section at your local library.

Follow the steps on the next two pages to learn how to use reference sources.

1 Choose a Reference Source

If you are looking up a place, an item, or an event, use an encyclopedia. If you are looking up a person, you can start with either a biographical dictionary or an encyclopedia.

2 Look up Your Subject

If you are using encyclopedias, they will probably be a set of **volumes,** or several individual books that make up a set. You will need to choose the right volume. Online and CD-ROM encyclopedias are often all together in one site or volume.

Use the index.

Look up the person, topic, place, or event in the index. The index is usually in the last book of the set. Online and CD-ROM sources will list an electronic index. Topics are listed alphabetically. People are listed alphabetically by last name.

The last name will be followed by a comma and then the first name. The index will give you the titles of the articles, the volume numbers or letters, and the pages. For example, suppose Martin Luther King, Jr. is in Volume 10, page 205. The index listing will look like this:

King, Martin Luther, Jr., 10: 205

Guide words will tell you if you are on the right page of an encyclopedia. The page for *segregation* might say *"Scotland-Senate"* at the top.

Look for related topics.

The index may list related topics under different key words. For example, *civil rights, segregation,* and *Montgomery bus boycott* are topics related to Martin Luther King, Jr.'s work.

Use the same steps to look up a person in a biographical dictionary. Biographical dictionaries often have only one book to look through, not a set of volumes.

3 Read the Article

Skim the article.

If you are looking for certain facts, skim the article to find them.

Reread and take notes.

Read the article a second time and write down important information in your own words.

4 Look for Other Sources

If you want more facts, look in the encyclopedia article for titles of other articles with useful information. Select which ones you want to look up.

You may also find a list of books about the subject at the end of the article. You might want to look for these books in your local library.

Protesters carry signs to show how they feel about segregation laws.

TIP There may be several index listings for the same last name, so be careful to look for the correct first name.

If you were to look up **segregation** in an encyclopedia index, you might find something like this. Notice the volume numbers, page numbers, and related topics.

segregation 15: 116.
> *of armed forces 1: 338*
> *laws against 9: 63*
> *King, Martin Luther, Jr. 10: 205*
> *March on Washington, 11: 96*
> *Montgomery bus boycott 11: 123*

When you find the volume with the articles about "King, Martin Luther, Jr.," the spine might read:

ket-lam

The letters on the spine show that the volume contains subjects starting with the letters "k-e-t" through "l-a-m." This is the right volume to use because the spelling of the last name "King" falls in between "ket" and "lam" alphabetically.

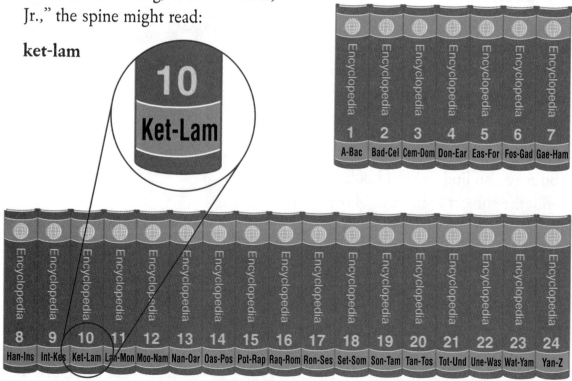

Use Reference Sources

From the list below, select one of the topics about the civil rights movement in the United States. Use reference sources to find out more about your topic of choice.

U.S. CIVIL RIGHTS MOVEMENT	
Rosa Parks	An African American woman who was arrested in 1955 in Montgomery, Alabama. Her crime: she refused to give her seat on a bus to a white man.
Montgomery bus boycott	A protest that followed Rosa Parks' arrest. Protesters refused to ride the buses in Montgomery, Alabama.
Martin Luther King, Jr.	A minister who became a major leader in the American civil rights movement of of the 1960s.
March on Washington	A march and demonstration in Washington, D.C., in 1963. Protesters demanded fair and equal treatment for all U.S. citizens.

TEST TIP On some tests you may need to choose which article would come first in an encyclopedia. Read all the answer choices. Compare the first letters of key words to see which letters come first in the alphabet.

Skill 29

Write a News Story

A Man, a Plan, a Canal: Panama!

Before cars and airplanes, cross-country railroads, and semi trucks, people traveled and sent goods by sea. Huge ships would travel long distances to take people and things where they needed to go. If you wanted to sail from New York to California in the year 1850, you would be on a boat for months. Your ship would have to go south from New York, all the way around the southern tip of South America, before heading north to California! This was a hard way to travel. But one man had a plan for a better way.

His name was George Goethals, and his plan was to build a canal, or human-made water passage, through the country of Panama. This canal would connect the Atlantic and Pacific oceans. By cutting across Central America, people traveling or shipping by boat would save time and money. The two-month journey from San Francisco to New York City could be done in just a few weeks. It was a great plan, but actually building the canal was a different story. There were many serious problems during the ten-year construction of the Panama Canal.

In the early 1900s, newspapers carried many stories about the building of the Panama Canal. A **news story** is a report on a current event. News stories are important sources of information for people all over the world.

A news story has these five parts:

The **headline** is the title. It tells the reader what the story is about. It should capture the reader's interest. The **byline** gives the name of the person who wrote the story. The **lead** paragraph introduces the most important facts. It often answers the questions Who? What? When? Where? Why? How?

The **body,** or **copy,** gives more detailed information about what happened. Sometimes people's ideas, opinions, and quotes are included in the body text.

The **ending** often tells the outcome of an event, how a problem was solved, or what could happen next.

Follow these steps to learn how to write a news story.

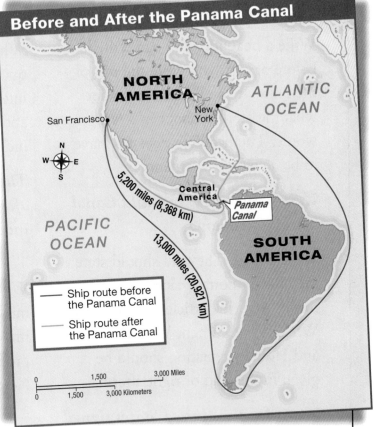

Before and After the Panama Canal

NORTH AMERICA

ATLANTIC OCEAN

San Francisco

New York

PACIFIC OCEAN

5,200 miles (8,368 km)

Central America

Panama Canal

13,000 miles (20,921 km)

SOUTH AMERICA

—— Ship route before the Panama Canal

—— Ship route after the Panama Canal

0   1,500   3,000 Miles
0   1,500   3,000 Kilometers

1 Gather Information

Find answers to the questions Who, What, When, Where, Why, and How. If you are at the event, watch and listen carefully. Take notes on what is happening. If you are not at the event, read about it and do research. Interview people who were or are involved in the event or who may have information about it.

141

2 Write a First Draft

Write a headline. You can write it before or after you write the rest of the draft. It should tell the reader what the story is about in a few words. The headline does not have to be a complete sentence.

U.S. Signs Treaty to Build Canal Through Panama

Write a lead. The lead should state the most important facts, and tell the reader what the article is about. The Who, What, When, Where, Why, and How information should be given in the lead or right after it.

Yesterday the United States signed a treaty with Panama. The treaty will allow the United States to build a canal through Panama between the Atlantic Ocean and the Pacific Ocean.

Write the body. Give thorough facts and details about the event you are covering. Tell the reader the Why, and more about the Who, What, Where, When, and How. Use direct quotes to make the article more interesting. For example, an article about the treaty with Panama might include this fact:

The treaty comes two weeks after Panama declared its independence from Colombia on November 3, 1903.

Write the ending. Your ending might state why the event is important. You could explain how a problem was solved, or what could happen next. Some stories end with a quotation predicting what will change because of the event.

Building the canal will be a long, difficult, and expensive project. The effort will be worth it, because the trip between the Atlantic and the Pacific will be so much shorter.

3 Revise and Edit

Read your draft. Did you include all the important facts and details? Does your story answer the questions Who, What, Where, When, Why, and How? If not, add the missing information. Are your facts correct? Are they presented clearly? Have a classmate, teacher, or family member read your first draft. Ask them to suggest ways you could improve your news story. Make any needed changes.

When you have made the other changes, check your spelling, capitalization, and punctuation.

TIPS

➤ Give the full name of each person quoted in your news story. Names should appear directly before or after each quotation.

➤ Be sure to give your article an interesting headline that will get the reader's attention.

4 Write the Final Copy

Write a clean final copy, including all the changes you made to your first draft. Add your byline by writing "By" and then your first and last names. Put the byline under the headline.

Boats first passed through the Panama Canal in the year 1914.

Read this news story about the Panama Canal.

Headline

Panama Canal Completed

Byline — *by Anna Gonzalez*

Lead — It took ten years, 350 million dollars, and many hardships, but builders have finally completed construction on the Panama Canal. The new canal connects the Atlantic and Pacific oceans by a human-made waterway through the Isthmus of Panama. The first ship traveled through it yesterday, August 15, 1914.

The Panama Canal

Body — Colonel George W. Goethals deserves much of the credit. As chief engineer of the U.S. Army Corps of Engineers, he directed the building of the canal. With his help, the builders managed to dam a large river and dig a channel through part of a mountain. Conditions were poor for the canal workers. Accidents and disease took almost 6,000 lives during the ten-year canal construction project.

Former U.S. President Theodore Roosevelt, through his agreement with Panama, made the building of the canal possible. Roosevelt supported Panama's revolution against Colombia, and Panama became independent from Colombian rule on November 3, 1903. The final treaty agreement for the Panama Canal was signed by the United States and Panama later that month. Construction began the following year, in 1904. **Body**

It took tens of thousands of workers to build the canal. Now ocean travel from New York to California will take less than half the time it did previously. Ocean travel between Europe and Asia will also be much faster and safer.

Ending

Write a News Story

Write a news story about a current event or one of the topics from the list below. If you write about an event in history, do research to write a news story that might have appeared in the past.

The Panama Canal

- Early French, English, and American interest in building a canal to connect the Atlantic and Pacific Oceans
- Panama's revolution and independence from Colombia
- Troubles in building the canal
- George Goethals, who directed the construction
- Why the armed forces wanted a canal through Panama
- Examples of how the Panama Canal has helped the United States or the world

TEST TIP

Sometimes you have to write a story or an article as part of a test. Be sure to give the most important and interesting information in the first few sentences of your story.

Skill 30

HOW TO

Write an Outline

Women on the Home Front

"We can do it!" This was the feeling that American women had about their important new work during World War II.

Before World War II, women had few job choices outside the home. Women had always cared for homes and children or held office jobs. Women rarely unloaded ships on the docks, drove trucks, or worked in steel mills. When the war called American men away from their homes and their jobs, women stepped in. They learned to build tanks and test weapons in the factories. They drove buses and delivered the mail. Women did whatever work was

We Can Do It!

needed while their husbands, sons, and brothers were away. These women proved to the nation that they were smart, strong, capable workers. The American workforce was forever changed.

Suppose you want to write about how World War II brought women into the workforce. You could use an outline to organize the many facts you would find. An **outline** is a written plan to organize notes and ideas into main topics and detailed subtopics. A **sentence outline** gives a complete sentence about each topic, subtopic, and detail.

1 Write the Outline Title

For example, the title *Working Women During World War II* would be written at the top of the page.

"THE GIRL HE LEFT BEHIND" IS STILL BEHIND HIM
She's a **WOW**
WOMAN ORDNANCE WORKER

2 Identify the Main Ideas

An outline should have at least two main ideas. In sentence outlines, **topic sentences** introduce main ideas. You can think of a topic sentence as the "title" for the subtopics and details that follow. Use a Roman numeral to number main topics on an outline.

I. During World War II, women were needed to fill many jobs.

TIP When writing an outline, write headings in "pairs." If you have a main topic signified by Roman numeral "I," then you must also have a main topic "II." If you have a subtopic "A," there must also be a subtopic "B."

3 Identify the Subtopics

A main idea may have two or more subtopics or none at all. **Subtopics** are like examples. They tell you what information is included about the main ideas. Use a capital letter to separate subtopics on the outline. Indent your subtopic.

I. During World War II, women were needed to fill many jobs.

A. The war created a need for more workers.

B. Men had left their jobs to join the armed forces.

Read the sample sentence outline below. Think about main ideas and subtopics.

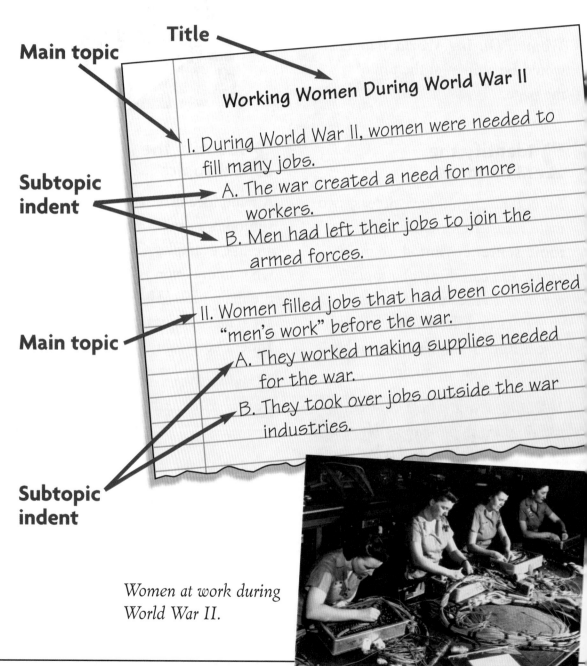

Main topic

Title

Subtopic indent

Working Women During World War II

I. During World War II, women were needed to fill many jobs.
   A. The war created a need for more workers.
   B. Men had left their jobs to join the armed forces.

II. Women filled jobs that had been considered "men's work" before the war.
   A. They worked making supplies needed for the war.
   B. They took over jobs outside the war industries.

Main topic

Subtopic indent

Women at work during World War II.

Write an Outline

Read the following sentences. Organize them into a title, two main ideas, and five subtopics on an outline.

- The U.S. Government and Women Workers During World War II
- The U.S. government announced on the radio that women workers were needed.
- The U.S. government provided child care for women workers.
- The U.S. government advertised in newspapers for women.
- The U.S. government tried to interest women in taking non-traditional jobs.
- The U.S. government raised women's wages.
- The U.S. government gave job training to women workers.
- The U.S. government made changes to help women join the workforce.

TEST TIP

On some tests you may need to organize sentences on an outline. Decide which choices are main ideas. These should be the topics on the outline. Then decide which choices are specific information about the main ideas. These should be the subtopics.

Skill 31

HOW TO

Write a Biography

Benjamin Franklin: Man of a Thousand Talents

Although he went to school only until age ten, he became a well-known printer, author, inventor, and scientist. Then he found time to become one of our country's greatest leaders. He was Benjamin Franklin!

This paragraph could be part of Benjamin Franklin's biography. A **biography** is the story of a person's life. A biography can be written of anyone, but many are about people who played important roles in history. Biographies tell facts, stories, and interesting details about people and their life's work. Biographies can make history come to life for the reader.

Benjamin Franklin

The **subject** of a biography is the person about whom the story is written. A biography may tell the subject's whole life story or only part of it. It may be written by a family member or friend of the subject, by a historian, or by any author who has studied the subject's life.

You can write a biography of a famous person, someone you know, or someone from your community. To learn how to write a biography, follow these steps.

STEPS IN **Writing a Biography**

1 Collect Information

Decide about whom you would like to write. You could write about a famous person, a classmate, or someone in your own family. Choose a person who is interesting.

Collect information about your subject. Find as many sources as possible.

Interview your subject.

If the subject is living, try to interview him or her. Write some questions you would like the subject to answer. If the subject is not living, you may be able to find interviews in an article written during the subject's lifetime.

Check reference sources.

If your subject is famous, you can find information about him or her in

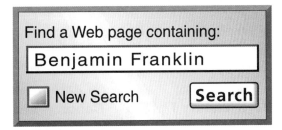

Find a Web page containing:

Benjamin Franklin

☐ New Search   Search

reference sources. Look in an encyclopedia to find highlights of the person's life. Encyclopedias come in book form, online, or on CD-ROM.

Check other sources.

Books or magazines may give more details than an encyclopedia. They may cover the subject's whole life, or part of the subject's life in detail.

Check online sources.

Many people in history have whole Web sites devoted to them. Sometimes a Web site on a period in history will give information about the famous people of the time.

Benjamin Franklin's Work
Notes: B. Franklin started publishing Poor Richard's
          Almanac in 1732.
Source: Brian Morgan, Great American Writers, 1999,
          page 412.

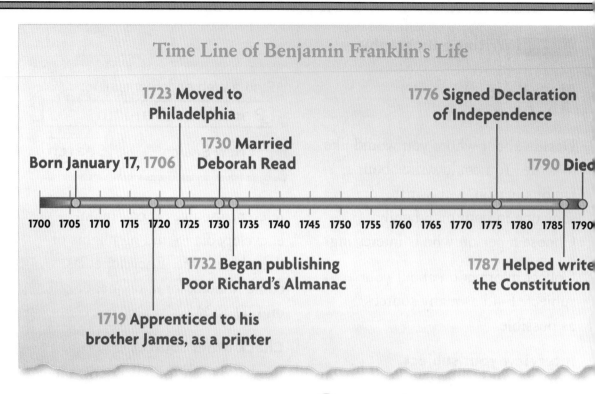

Time Line of Benjamin Franklin's Life

1723 Moved to Philadelphia

1776 Signed Declaration of Independence

1730 Married Deborah Read

Born January 17, 1706

1790 Died

1700 1705 1710 1715 1720 1725 1730 1735 1740 1745 1750 1755 1760 1765 1770 1775 1780 1785 1790

1732 Began publishing Poor Richard's Almanac

1787 Helped write the Constitution

1719 Apprenticed to his brother James, as a printer

Take notes.

When you find information you can use, read it carefully and take notes. Write down where you read the information. Include the title of the source, author, date of publication, and page number. If you use a quote, copy it exactly and then write down who said the quote and the source.

2 Organize Your Information

You can organize your information in many ways. Suppose you are telling the events of the subject's life in order, from their birth to their death. You can create a time line and put important events and dates on it. Divide the time line into the periods of a person's life. For example, you could divide Benjamin Franklin's life into three periods: Before the Revolutionary War, During the Revolutionary War, and After the Revolutionary War.

3 Write a First Draft

Be sure each paragraph has a topic sentence and supporting details. Your biography should make clear why the subject is interesting or famous. You might want to begin by telling why your subject is important, describing an important moment in your subject's life, or by using a quote. Use quotes from your subject or from someone who knew them. Quotes make a biography more lively and personal.

4 Revise and Edit

Read your draft. Does it explain what kind of person your subject is or was? Will the information be clear to your reader? Is it well organized in time order or by topic? Ask your classmates, family, or teacher to read your draft. Ask them if your biography makes them understand why your subject is important. Ask if they have suggestions about how you could improve your biography.

Once you have checked the facts, the order, and the wording, proofread your draft. Check for correct capitalization, punctuation, spelling, and grammar. Mark the changes that you need to make to your draft. If you are using a computer, you may want to use the spell-check feature.

5 Make a Final Copy

If you are using a computer, you can make changes directly to your draft document. If you are writing by hand, neatly copy your revised biography onto a clean sheet of paper.

TIPS

➤ **Use the tables of contents and indexes from reference sources to find important facts about your subject.**

➤ **Index cards are a good place to write your notes and keep them organized.**

Read this sample biography about Benjamin Franklin.

Benjamin Franklin's Early Life

Quotes make introduction more lively

→ "I do not remember when I could not read," said Benjamin Franklin. He did not go to school until age eight, but by then he was already reading well. At age ten, he was taken out of school and put to work in his father's business.

Topic sentence

→ Franklin was born in Boston on January 17, 1706. His father, Josiah Franklin, made soap and candles. People thought Josiah Franklin was very wise. Boston leaders came to ask what he thought about important matters. By listening as they talked, Benjamin was exposed to many ideas and facts about business, law, politics, education, and the world around him.

Supporting details

Topic sentence

→ Benjamin's education did not stop when he left school. "From a child I was fond of reading," he wrote, "and all the little money that came into my hands was ever laid out in books." At age 12, Benjamin went to work for his brother James, who was a printer and published a newspaper.

Supporting details

Write a Biography

From the list below, pick one of the people who played an important part in the American Revolution. Write a biography about an important part of the subject's life.

Heroes of the Revolution

- Samuel Adams, 1722–1803. Patriotic speaker and writer. Member of both Continental Congresses, signer of the Declaration of Independence, governor of Massachusetts.

- George Rogers Clark, 1752–1818. Military leader and frontiersman. Led raids on British troops during the Revolutionary War.

- John Paul Jones, 1747–1792. An officer in the American navy during the American Revolution. Famous for raids on the British.

- Paul Revere, 1735–1818. Silversmith and American Revolutionary hero. On April 18, 1775, he rode to warn that the British troops were coming to Lexington and Concord, Massachusetts.

- Haym Salomon, 1740–1785. Banker and American patriot. Spied on British for America. Made loans to the government to help support the American Revolution.

TEST TIP On some tests you may need to write about famous people. When writing about people, be sure to capitalize their first and last names.

HOW TO

Prepare an Oral Report

Alaska: The Last Frontier

The name Alaska comes from the Aleut Indian word *Alyeska*, meaning "The Great Land." Not only is Alaska the largest state in the United States, it is also a kind of "last frontier." Much of Alaska's land remains unsettled, even to this day. It is home to both North America's tallest mountain and its deepest ocean trench. In winter, Alaskan skies are dark for months on end. During the months of June and July, the sun shines nearly around the clock. For this reason, Alaska has the nickname "Land of the Midnight Sun."

This information would be interesting to include in an oral report about Alaska. A **report** is a presentation, spoken or in writing, about a single topic. Most reports include information about real people, places, or events. An **oral report** is a report delivered in person to a live audience.

Doing a report about one of the 50 states can help you learn about U.S. history and geography.

Midnight at Kodiak Island, Alaska

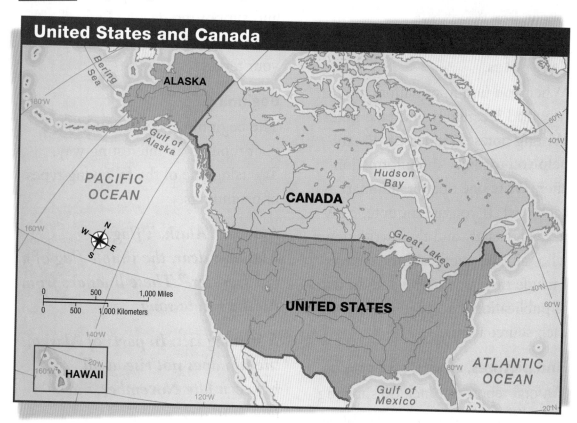

United States and Canada

1 Find Sources of Information

Find as many different sources of information as you can. You may be able to interview an expert. Library books, magazines, audio tapes, video tapes, and Web sites are full of interesting information.

Check reference sources.

Encyclopedias give general information about topics. They come in book form, online, or on CD-ROM. Atlases have detailed maps and facts about geography.

2 Collect Information

Gather the facts you need for your report. You might start by writing questions you would like to answer. Then search your sources of information for answers.

State Flag of Alaska

Take notes.

When you find information you can use, read it carefully and take notes. Writing notes on index cards can help you organize the information later. Write one note or summary on each card. If you use a quote, copy it down exactly and then write down who said the quote and the source. Include the name of the author, date of publication, and page number for each source used.

Find pictures, charts, and graphs.

An oral report can include showing and telling. Photos and illustrations make reports more interesting. Charts and graphs are good ways to present facts and figures.

3 Prepare Your Report

First, organize your information. What do you want to show or tell? Decide which facts are most important to include in your oral report. It may help to write an outline of the main topics, subtopics, and supporting details. Prepare a beginning, middle, and ending for your report.

Beginning

The beginning should introduce your topic in an interesting way. Try using one of the following types of beginnings.

A quote: *"Alaska's flag, to Alaskans dear, the simple flag of a last frontier." These lines are from Alaska's state song.*

A startling fact: *In parts of Alaska, the sun does not rise at all between late November and late January.*

A story: *On my trip to Alaska, I was surprised to learn the state sport is "dog mushing," which is racing dog sleds. I'll never forget my first dog-sled race.*

An interesting question: *In which state can you see the sun shining at midnight in summer? The "Land of the Midnight Sun," Alaska!*

Middle

The middle should give more facts about your topic. This is the main "body" of your report. Decide what pictures, charts, or examples to show. Create your own charts and pictures if you need them. Using your own artwork will make your report more unique, interesting, and fun.

"Dog mushing," Alaska's state sport

Ending

The ending should tell why the subject is important to you, your audience, the community, or the world. The last two or three sentences could summarize main points from your report. The ending should sound final and complete.

TIPS

➤ **Write your notes large enough and clearly enough that you can quickly glance at the facts as you present.**

➤ **Use an audio tape or video tape while you practice giving your report. Listen to or view the tape and decide if you need to make changes.**

4 Rehearse Your Report

Practice giving your oral report. After you have practiced alone, you may want to do your report for family or friends. Practice these public speaking skills.

- Introduce yourself and your topic.

- Give your report in a strong voice and speak clearly.

- Look at the audience as much as possible.

- Keep going even if you make a mistake.

After you have practiced in front of an audience, ask them to suggest improvements. Make any changes you might need, then practice again.

Read the sample note cards below. Notice the beginning, the middle, and the summary statement at the end.

Beginning

Title: A Short History of Alaska, America's 49th State

Do you know that in 1867, a few newspapers called Alaska "Seward's Folly"? Secretary of State William H. Seward persuaded U.S. government to buy Alaska from Russia. Some thought this was a bad decision. If the U.S. had not bought it, Alaska might be part of Russia today.

Middle

In 1896, gold was discovered in Alaska's Klondike area. A gold rush began. People came from all over the world in hopes of finding gold and getting rich. Some did succeed, but most were disappointed. Mining gold in the frozen mountains of Alaska was hard work. Temperatures in Alaska can go below -70°F. Some miners lost their lives because of harsh weather.

Ending

Alaska is called our "last frontier" because it still has many untapped resources and unsettled land. Had Alaska's many resources been known about in 1867, nobody would have called Alaska "Seward's folly."

Preparing an Oral Report

Prepare an oral report about the history or culture of your own state. Select one of the topics below.

- Your state's economy and resources
- Your state's geography and climate
- Your state's native peoples
- The history of your state's state sport, state song, state motto, or state bird
- The history of your state's early European settlers
- The art and music of your state

TEST TIP Sometimes you need to give an oral report as part of a test. Preparing your report in advance will help you do well on the oral part of the test.

Chart and Graph Skills

HOW TO

Read a Time Line

Dates in American History

The first European-American colony, Jamestown, Virginia, was settled in 1607. Then in 1620, settlers landed in Plymouth, Massachusetts. Maryland was settled in 1634, and Pennsylvania in 1681. The last colony settled by Europeans was Georgia in 1732, more than 100 years after the first.

When you study history, you need to learn when things happened.

Sometimes history writers help you make sense of multiple dates and events by showing them on a time line. A **time line** is a type of diagram. It lists dates and events along a line, in the order that they took place.

Some time lines are written across a page, like the one shown below. These are read from left to right, in the same way you read a sentence. The earliest dates appear at the left end of the time line. More recent dates are toward the right end.

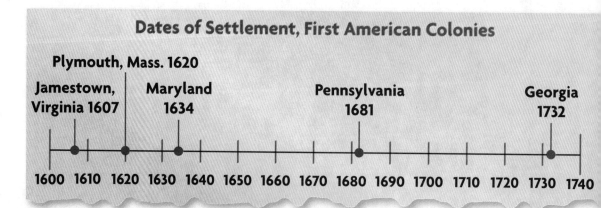

Dates of Settlement, First American Colonies

Plymouth, Mass. 1620

Jamestown, Virginia 1607 — Maryland 1634 — Pennsylvania 1681 — Georgia 1732

1600 1610 1620 1630 1640 1650 1660 1670 1680 1690 1700 1710 1720 1730 1740

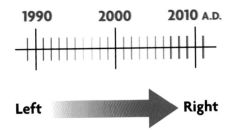

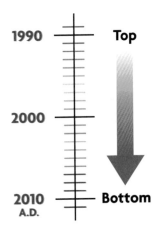

Other time lines are written in a vertical line (up and down) on a page. These are read either from top to bottom or from bottom to top. Pay close attention to how dates are written on vertical time lines. Some show earlier dates at the top of the time line, some show earlier dates at the bottom.

The distance between the events on the time line shows about how much time passed between the events.

Time lines are divided into time periods. **Time periods** are portions of time. They can show long periods, even millions of years. They can also show very short time periods, such as a few hours or days.

You can learn how to read time lines by following the steps on the next two pages.

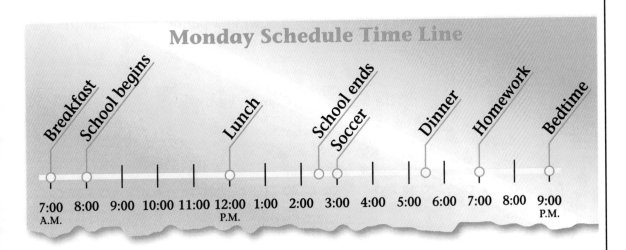

1 Read the Title

Read the title of the time line to find out what time period is being shown. Check to see if the time line covers hours, days, months, years, hundreds of years, or millions of years. The amount of time covered by the time line is important to understand. For example, if the time line covers a period of millions of years, weeks and months will not be marked along the time line.

The title of the time line below tells you that the time period being shown is one year.

2 See How Time Is Divided

Some time lines may be divided into time segments of one day, one month, or one year in each segment. Others may be divided into time periods of ten thousand years in each segment. Look closely at the time line to see how time segments are marked. Are the segments consistent, or do the marks show different blocks of time? Look at the numbers to understand how time is divided on the time line. The time line below shows the months of a year. This time line is divided into twelve segments, each segment showing a period of one month.

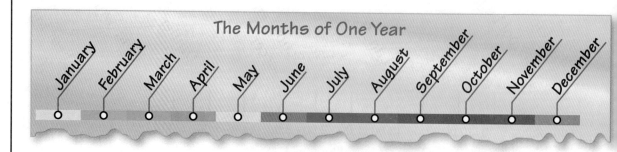

The Months of One Year

January February March April May June July August September October November December

Major Battles of the American Revolution

Battles of Lexington and Concord	1775
Battles at Trenton and White Plains	1776
Battles at Saratoga and Brandywine	1777
Battles at Monmouth and Savannah	1778
Battle at Augusta	1779
Battles at Charleston and King's Mountain	1780
Battle of Yorktown	1781

3 Look for Dates and Events

Read to see which events are covered on the time line. Look for ways the events are related. Does the time line have a theme, such as "Events During the School Year"? Read the time line on this page. You will notice that the words on the time line give the names of battles. The dates tell you when the battles happened. By reading the title, you will see that these battles were part of the Revolutionary War.

4 Look at the Order of Events

Look at the order in which events take place. It is possible that some earlier events are causes of later events. Notice the order that events appear on the time line. This can help you to understand relationships between events in history.

5 Note Time Between Events

The distance between the events on a time line will give you an idea of how much time passed between them. For example, the time line on this page shows that six years passed between the first major battle of the Revolutionary War in 1775, and the last battle in 1781.

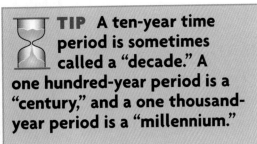

TIP A ten-year time period is sometimes called a "decade." A one hundred-year period is a "century," and a one thousand-year period is a "millennium."

Read the time line below. Notice the order of events and how much time passed between events.

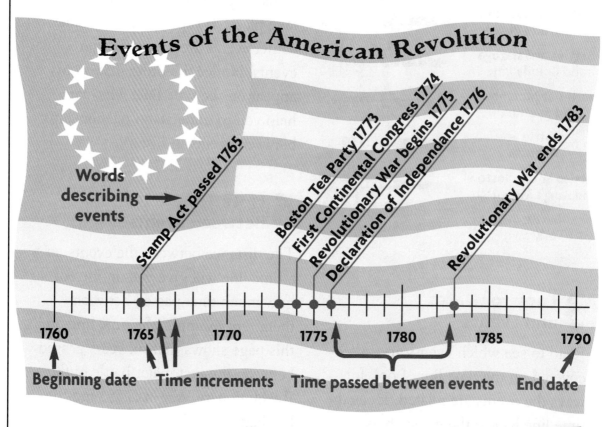

Events of the American Revolution

Words describing events →

Stamp Act passed 1765

Boston Tea Party 1773

First Continental Congress 1774

Revolutionary War begins 1775

Declaration of Independance 1776

Revolutionary War ends 1783

1760   1765   1770   1775   1780   1785   1790

Beginning date   **Time increments**   **Time passed between events**   **End date**

"The Boston Tea Party" was one of the first big events in the American Revolution.

USE THIS SKILL

Read a Time Line

Read the time line below. Use information on the time line to answer the questions on this page.

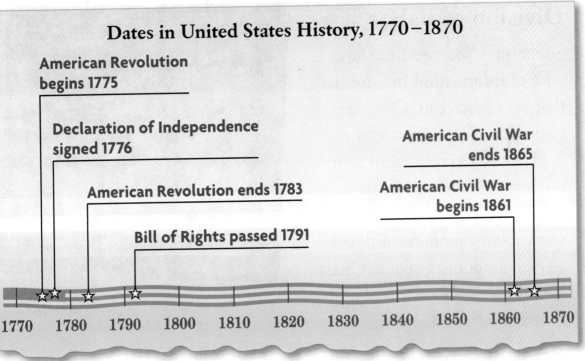

Dates in United States History, 1770–1870

American Revolution begins 1775

Declaration of Independence signed 1776

American Revolution ends 1783

Bill of Rights passed 1791

American Civil War ends 1865

American Civil War begins 1861

1770 1780 1790 1800 1810 1820 1830 1840 1850 1860 1870

1. In what year did the American Revolution begin?

2. How many years did the American Revolution last?

3. When was the Declaration of Independence signed?

4. How many years did the American Civil War last?

TEST TIP On some tests you may need to read a time line. Look carefully at the dates and events. Compare the answer choices to the time line.

Skill 34

HOW TO

Make a Chart

Division of Labor

Sometimes you need to show a lot of information in a format that is easy to read. One way to do this is to make a chart. A **chart** is a graphic tool used to show information in an organized way. A chart can show a large amount of data in a small amount of space. Charts make it possible to compare different items easily.

This auto worker specializes in doing one job only.

Suppose you are learning about how the United States is able to produce many cars. Our country can do this because each worker does not make a whole car. Instead there is a **division of labor.** This means the big job of making a car is divided into many smaller jobs. Each worker specializes. She or he does one job only. This way, workers get to be

very good at what they do, and many cars can be built in a short time.

To help explain this idea, you could make a chart showing the many jobs there are in the process of making a car. Here are some steps you can take to make a chart.

1 Choose a Title

Look over the information you have gathered. Think of a few simple words to describe that information. That should be your chart title.

2 Choose Headings

A chart has rows and columns. Rows go across the chart. Columns go down the chart. Decide which category of your information should go in the rows and which category should go in the columns. Usually the rows name the items that will be compared. The columns give different information about each item.

A Simple Chart

Row →

Column

TIPS

➤ **You don't have to use complete sentences in your chart.**

➤ **If you have a computer, you can use it to make a chart.**

3 Draw Your Chart

Write headings to tell what information is in each row and column. Row headings should be written at the beginning of each row on your chart. Column headings should be written at the top of each column. Then draw lines between the rows and the columns to create boxes. Fill in each box with the correct information.

4 Check Your Chart

Look over your chart. Read it from left to right across each row. Then read it from top to bottom down each column. Check to see that you have placed the right information in each box.

Read the chart below. Think about how the chart shows information about how the big job of making a car is divided into many smaller jobs.

Chart title

Column

Division of Labor—Building a Car

Row →

Jobs	What They Do
Press operator	Operate machines that make pieces of frame
Body welder	Connect pieces of the frame together
Spray paint operator	Operate primer and paint sprayers
Glass installer	Fit glass for windows and windshield
Dashboard installer	Attach the dashboard to inside of frame
Carpet and trim installer	Install carpeting, electric wires, and interior
Seat installer	Attach seats to floor of car
Mechanical unit fitters	Install engine and other mechanical parts
Wheel installer	Mount wheels and tires
Door installer	Attach doors to frame
Finisher	Wash, wax, and detail car

Make a Chart

Read the passage below. Make a chart to organize the school jobs described in the passage.

Jobs in My School

One hundred years ago in the days of one-room schools a teacher had to do everything—teach all the subjects, clean the classroom, and warm up student lunches in the winter. Today there are many jobs in my school. Each person specializes in doing just one thing. That way, everyone can do what he or she does best. This makes our school more efficient. Ms. Rodriguez is the school principal. She is in charge of the school. Mr. Lewis is the cook in the cafeteria. He cooks the lunches. Ms. Tamura is the computer teacher. She teaches every grade how to use our computers. Mr. Geisler is the art teacher. He teaches art to everyone. Ms. Linn is the librarian. She runs the library. Mr. Malik is the custodian. He is in charge of keeping the school clean and making repairs.

TEST TIP

You may be asked to read a chart on a test. If there are many rows, line up a pencil or a piece of paper along each row as a guide to help you read across.

Skill 35

Make a Bar Graph

Comparing Prices

When you buy an item, you want to know that you are not paying too much for it. One way to make sure you are getting good value for your money is to compare prices. It is helpful to compare information in an easy-to-read format. One way to do this is with a bar graph.

A **bar graph** uses numbers, lines, and bars to compare two or more things. Bar graphs are a good tool to use to compare and contrast data. For example, you might need to compare the prices of various brands of an item. A bar graph displays this information so that it is easy to see.

Here are some steps you can follow to create a simple bar graph.

1 Collect Information

Decide what you want to compare and contrast. Collect the facts and figures you will need to explain your topic. For example, if you were studying the prices of different brands of dog food, you could go to a store and write down each brand name and its price.

2 Choose a Title

Choose a title that describes the information you will show in your bar graph.

STEPS IN Making a Bar Graph

3 Draw Your Bar Graph

A bar graph shows information across the bottom and along the left or right side. The line at the bottom shows categories to be compared. The line at the side shows amounts. Choose labels for the amounts and categories. Decide how you will show amounts. Enter the range of numbers you will use from smallest to largest. Fill in the missing numbers using a ruler to mark off even spaces between them. Now make bars on your graph to show your information. Add a caption if you want to explain more about your bar graph.

4 Check Your Bar Graph

When you are finished, look over your bar graph. Read the title and labels. Then check each bar to be sure it ends at the right number. The amounts represented by the bars on your graph show contrasts, such as different prices.

Comparing Dog Food Prices

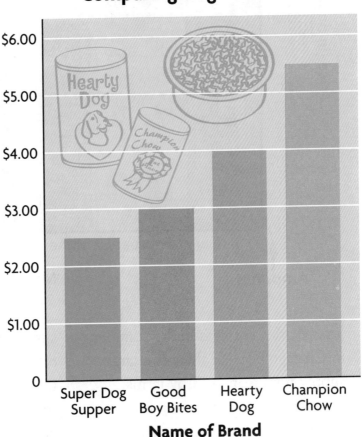

Making a Bar Graph

Read the bar graph below to see if strawberries cost more in summer months than in winter months.

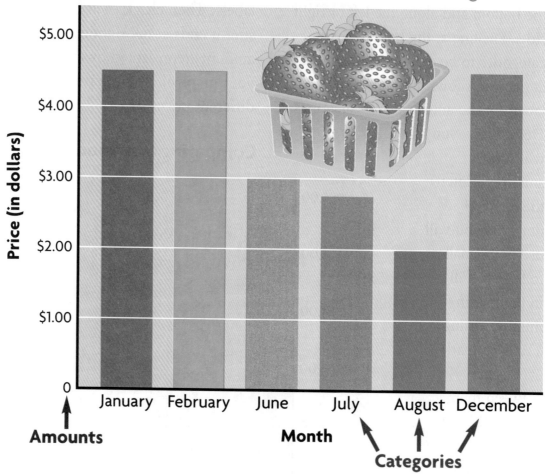

Title ➡ Cost of a Pint of Strawberries in Chicago

Amounts

Month

Categories

Strawberries cost less in the summer in Chicago because there is a large supply from many nearby farms. Strawberries cost more in the winter because there is a much smaller supply available from Florida and other places far away. It costs more to get strawberries and other fruits from far away places than from nearby farms.

Make a Bar Graph

Read the passage below. Then make a bar graph showing the three different movie admission prices at three different theaters.

Movie Prices

Sara noticed that movie admission prices fall after a movie has been out a long time. She went to see a movie version of her favorite book, *Princess of the Prairie,* when it first opened on her birthday in October. It cost $7 to see it at the fancy movie theater at the mall. In November, Sara saw that the movie was playing at a smaller theater in her neighborhood where the admission price was $5. In February, Sara noticed that the movie was now showing at a local "discount theater" for $1.

TEST TIP

You may be asked to read a bar graph on a test. Use a pencil or a piece of paper as a guide to help you see where the bars end. When a bar ends just before a line or just after a line you must estimate its value.

Skill 36
HOW TO
Make a Line Graph

Graphing Changing Prices

Have you ever noticed that the prices of items can go up and down? Sometimes a new product will have a high price at first, then get less expensive as time goes by. On the other hand, when a product suddenly becomes very popular or hard to find, the price often goes up. These changes in price are affected by supply and demand.

Quantity supplied means the amount of a product or service that is for sale at any one time. **Quantity demanded** means the amount of a product or service that people want to buy at any one time. Changes in demand, supply, or both can result in changes in selling price.

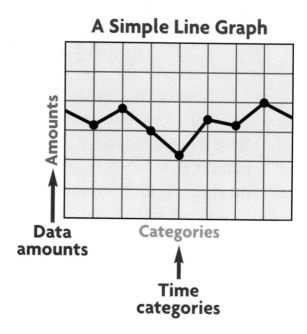

A Simple Line Graph

When you want to show how something such as price changes over a month or year or another period of time, you can use a line graph. A **line graph** uses dots connected by a line to show how something changes over time.

Follow the steps on the next page to learn how to create a line graph.

1 Choose a Title

Decide what information you want to show in your line graph. Choose a title that tells what you will show on the graph.

2 Set Up the Line Graph

Decide what time categories you will use. Also decide what kinds of data will be shown. Usually the left side of the graph tells the amounts and the bottom tells the time categories. Choose labels for these two sides of your graph. Labels will make the graph clear and easy to read.

TIP You can use a computer to make your line graph, or just use a ruler, a pencil, and graph paper.

3 Draw Your Line Graph

Decide how you will show amounts. Begin with a zero at the bottom left of your graph. Then look at the largest number in your information. Put that number at the top left. Use a ruler to mark off even spaces between the zero and your largest number. Now fill in the numbers. Draw straight lines from the numbers across your graph. Then draw straight lines from your categories at the bottom of your graph to the top.

4 Plot the Information

Place a dot on the graph showing where each amount and each time period meet. Then draw a line connecting your dots. Double-check each dot to be sure it is placed at the right number.

EXAMPLE OF Making a Line Graph

Read the line graph below to see how many children's bikes the Best Bike Company sold each month. Think about why more bikes were sold in some months than in others.

Title →

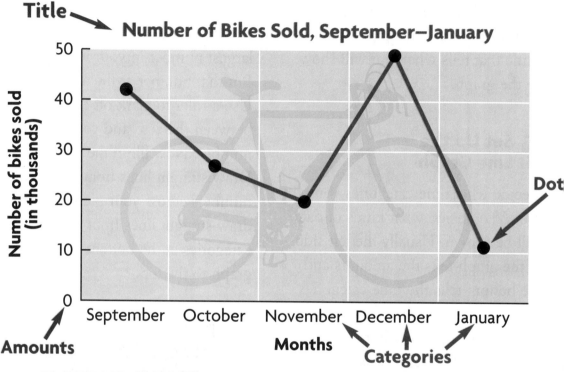

Number of Bikes Sold, September–January

Number of bikes sold (in thousands)

Amounts →

Months

Categories

Dot →

The Best Bike Company sold more bikes in September and December and fewer in other months. This happened because the demand for bikes went up when school started and during the holiday season. **Demand** means the amount of an item people are willing and able to buy at different prices.

Make a Line Graph

Use the information in the following passage to complete the line graph below.

A change in demand can make prices change. When many people wanted bikes in September, the company sold its bikes for $75. In October and November, when fewer people wanted bikes, the company lowered the price to $70 to try to attract business. In December the company raised its price back to $75 because demand for bikes went up during the holiday season. In January, after the holiday season ended, the company lowered the price to $50.

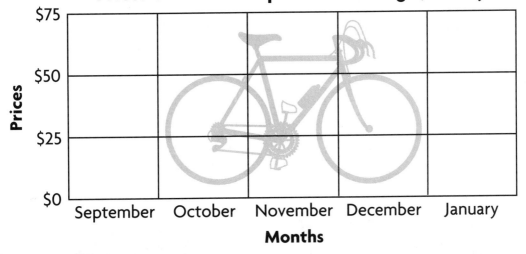

Prices of Bikes in September through January

| | September | October | November | December | January |

TEST TIP **You may be asked to read a line graph on a test. Be sure to check the label to see what units the numbers are in—thousands, millions, or other large units.**

Skill 37

Read a Circle Graph

Getting a Piece of the Pie

Have you ever been in a situation in which your friends or classmates all wanted something, but there was only so much of it to go around? The item would have to be divided into parts so that everyone could have a share. Making sure that everyone gets a fair share can be difficult. Using an organizing tool can be very helpful.

Sometimes you need to show how something can be divided into parts. You can do this with a circle graph. A **circle graph** is an organizing tool shaped like a circle divided into sections. The sections are used to show different parts, or amounts, of

a whole. Circle graphs can be used to show how money, objects, or even groups of people can be divided. Looking at the sizes of the different sections is a quick and easy way to compare information.

Suppose your class was working on several products that used paper but you had only a limited supply. How should the paper be divided? A circle graph could be used to show how the supply of paper was divided. Follow the steps to learn how to read a circle graph.

A Circle Graph

Sections

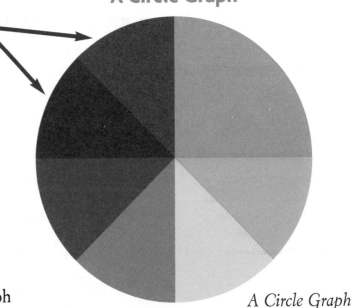

A Circle Graph

1 Look at the Title

The title will tell you what data is being shown in the circle graph.

2 Read Each Label

Each section of the circle graph should have a label telling you what part of the whole the section is. Sometimes each section has a different color or pattern. If so, there may be a key showing you what each color or pattern means. The sections will often be labeled with numbers.

3 Compare the Sections

Look over each section of the circle graph to see which is the largest, the smallest, and any size in between. Notice how the sizes of the sections relate to one another. These sizes show different amounts or parts of a whole. The largest section of the circle graph represents the largest amount of the whole. The smallest section on the circle graph shows the smallest part of the whole.

TIP Sometimes a circle chart is called a pie chart because it looks like a pie cut into pieces.

Look at the circle graph below to see how the class divided a limited amount of paper between groups.

In My Class of 24 students:

12 students need paper for Social Studies projects

2 students need paper for Art projects

4 students need paper for Science projects

6 students need paper for Language Arts projects

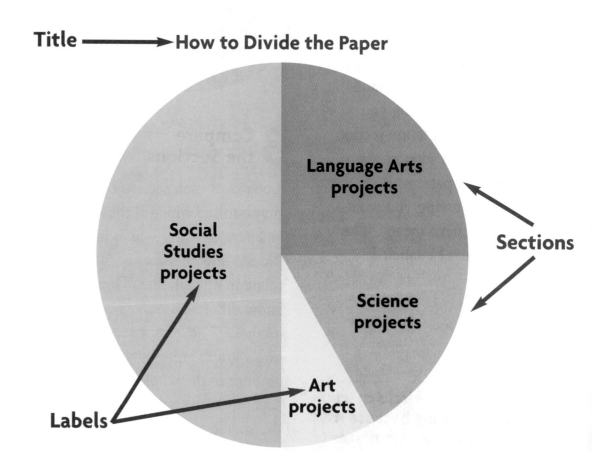

Title ⟶ **How to Divide the Paper**

Language Arts projects

Social Studies projects

Science projects

Art projects

Sections

Labels

USE THIS SKILL

Read a Circle Graph

Read the circle graph and answer the questions below.

1. What is the total class budget?

2. Will more of the class budget be spent on field trips or on software?

3. Which activity will get more of the budget: the school play or the holiday party?

4. Which two activities will get the smallest parts of the budget?

5. Which activity will get the largest part of the budget?

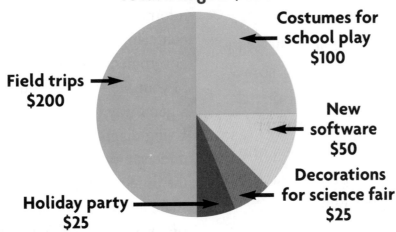

How Class Budget Will Be Spent
Total Budget: $400

Costumes for school play $100

Field trips $200

New software $50

Decorations for science fair $25

Holiday party $25

TEST TIP
Some tests may ask you to read a circle graph. Pay attention to the keywords in or on the graph. This can help you understand what the graph is showing.

HOW TO

Read a Diagram

Federal, State, and Local Governments

Your life is affected every day by laws. The federal government makes some of those laws, and state and local governments make others. For example, the state government sets up general rules for elementary education. The state sets the rules for electing some school boards. A school board is a form of local government. The school board decides how much money to give to each school in your town.

State governments have limits. The U.S. Constitution, part of our national law, says that all people have equal rights. So, the state cannot educate some children but not others. State governments have the power to make some laws, but they must still obey the U.S. Constitution.

When you read about government powers, you are given new information that may seem confusing. Thinking about how government powers affect something in your life, such as your school, is a good way to understand them. Using diagrams can also help you understand new concepts, such as the differences between national, state, and local governments. A **diagram** is a graphic tool used to show and explain information. The **title** tells what the diagram shows. **Labels** name different parts of the diagram.

There are many different kinds of diagrams. A **picture diagram** uses pictures to show how things work or how they are related to each other. A **Venn diagram** uses two overlapping circles to compare and contrast information. A **line diagram** uses lines, words, and symbols to show relationships between ideas. Below is an example of a picture diagram showing some ways that state governments make laws for education.

The steps on the next two pages can help you read three different types of diagrams: picture diagrams, Venn diagrams, and line diagrams.

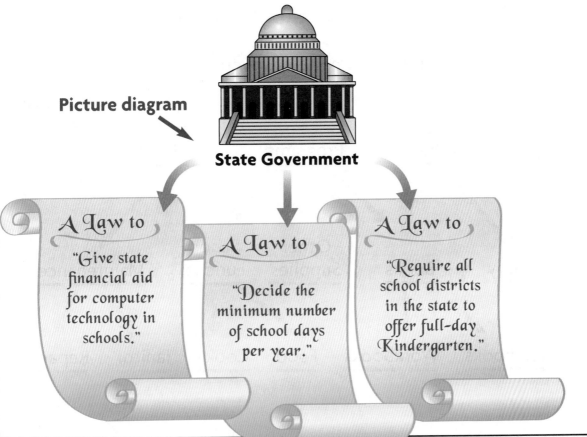

Governing Education

Picture diagram

State Government

A Law to
"Give state financial aid for computer technology in schools."

A Law to
"Decide the minimum number of school days per year."

A Law to
"Require all school districts in the state to offer full-day Kindergarten."

Reading a Diagram

1 Read the Title

Most diagrams have a title or heading. The heading or title of the diagram will tell you what information is being shown.

2 Read the Labels

Labels explain the parts of the diagram. Some kinds of diagrams have pointer lines or arrows going from labels to parts of the diagram. Other kinds of diagrams just have labels placed directly on the diagram. Make sure you read and understand all of the labels.

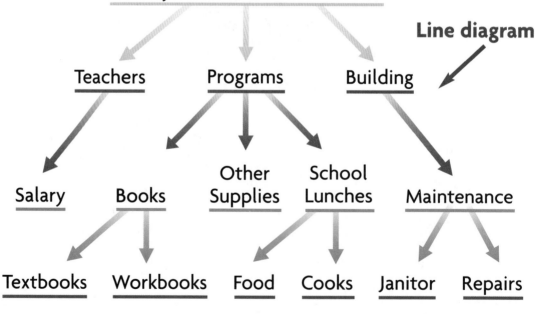

Forest City School Budget

Money From State Government

Line diagram

Teachers   Programs   Building

Salary   Books   Other Supplies   School Lunches   Maintenance

Textbooks   Workbooks   Food   Cooks   Janitor   Repairs

3 Study the Information Shown

What can you learn from the diagram? Diagrams can show how things are made or put together, or how things work. Diagrams can also show how parts of a system are related to one another. Diagrams are easiest to understand when they are read completely, as a whole.

Read all of the information shown in a diagram, not just one part.

The Venn diagram below shows state government decisions, local school board decisions, and decisions they both share. The shared decisions are in the overlapping parts of the circles.

Who Makes Education Decisions?

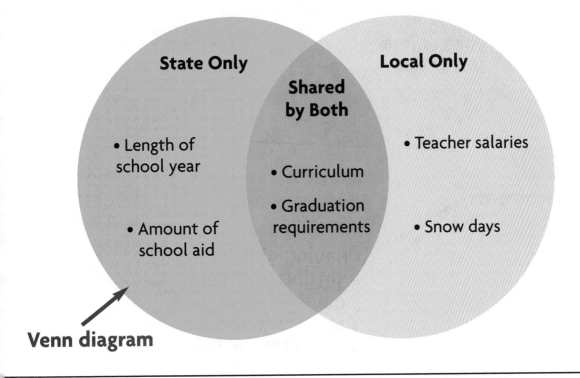

State Only

- Length of school year

- Amount of school aid

Shared by Both

- Curriculum

- Graduation requirements

Local Only

- Teacher salaries

- Snow days

Venn diagram

EXAMPLE OF Reading a Diagram

Look at the diagram below showing state and federal government powers. See how one student used this diagram to help complete this assignment: **List three powers of the state government.**

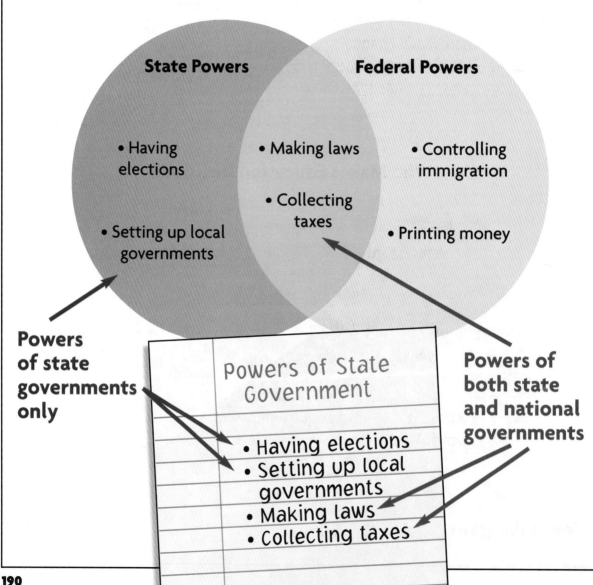

Division of Powers

State Powers

- Having elections

- Setting up local governments

- Making laws

- Collecting taxes

Federal Powers

- Controlling immigration

- Printing money

Powers of state governments only

Powers of both state and national governments

Powers of State Government

- Having elections
- Setting up local governments
- Making laws
- Collecting taxes

Read a Diagram

Read the diagram about branches of the U.S. government. Use the diagram to answer the questions below.

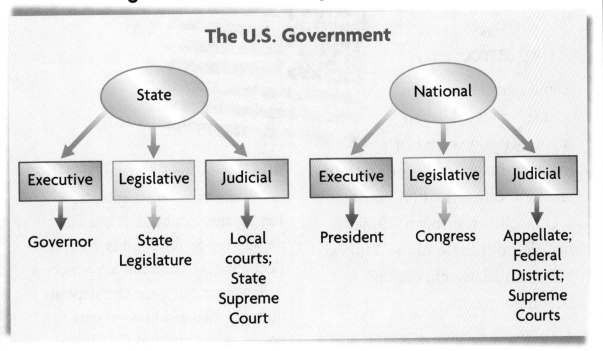

The U.S. Government

1. What is the chief executive officer of the state called?

2. What is the lawmaking body for the state?

3. What is the chief executive officer of the nation called?

4. What is the lawmaking body for the nation?

TEST TIP On some tests you may be asked to read a diagram. First read the title and labels. Be sure you understand the diagram before answering questions about it.

Skill 39
HOW TO
Read a Flowchart

"I Pledge Allegiance . . ."

Some people are born citizens of the United States. If you were born in this country or if your parents are U.S. citizens, then you were a U.S. citizen at birth. Other people immigrate to the United States and later choose to become citizens.

A **citizen** is a native or legal resident of a country. Citizens have the rights and responsibilities provided by the laws of the country. They must obey these laws and stay loyal to the government of their country.

People who come to a new country to live are called **immigrants.** Immigrants can become citizens of the United States or other countries. Becoming a citizen is a long process. A flowchart can show the steps an immigrant takes in the process of becoming a citizen of the United States. **Flowcharts** are graphic tools that show the steps of a process in order. Labels, arrows, and illustrations can add information to flowcharts.

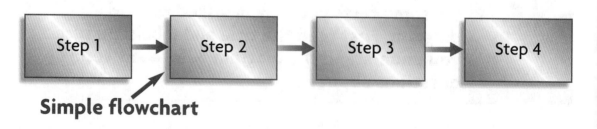

Simple flowchart

1 Look at the Title

The title will tell you what information the flowchart shows.

TIP Flowcharts can show movement from left to right, from top to bottom, or in a circle pattern.

2 Look at the Steps

Look at the number of steps in the process. Find where the process begins and ends. Read the flowchart carefully, making sure you understand each step.

3 Follow the Steps in Order

Arrows and labels can help you follow the order of the steps in a process. Be sure you understand each step before moving on to read the next one.

Basic Steps to U.S. Citizenship

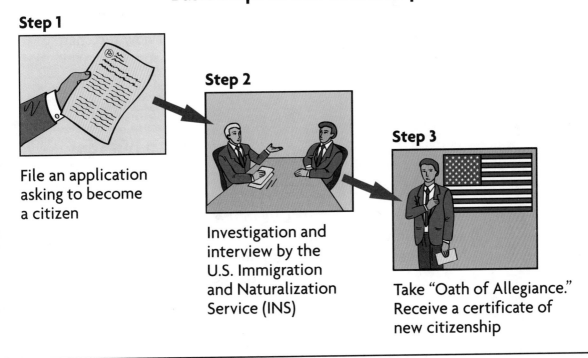

Step 1

File an application asking to become a citizen

Step 2

Investigation and interview by the U.S. Immigration and Naturalization Service (INS)

Step 3

Take "Oath of Allegiance." Receive a certificate of new citizenship

The Statue of Liberty

Flowcharts come in every shape, size, and color. They often include numbers, artwork, or photographs. Flowcharts can be found in instruction booklets, in news articles, in textbooks, and even in sports game plans.

Some flowcharts may seem complicated or crowded with information, but they will make sense if you read them carefully. Read the title of the flowchart, notice the number of steps and the order of the steps, and read the information in each step. The flowchart below should be read from left to right. Both the step numbers and the arrows show you how the chart should be read.

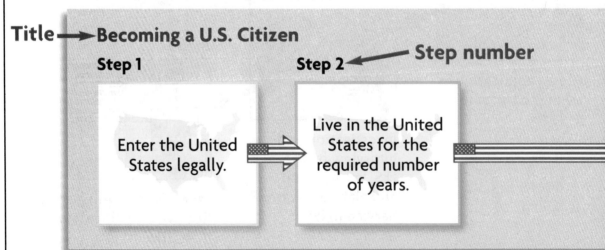

Title ——▶ **Becoming a U.S. Citizen**

Step 1 **Step 2** ◀—— **Step number**

Enter the United States legally. ⟹ Live in the United States for the required number of years.

Read the flowchart below to see the steps an immigrant must take to become a citizen of the United States.

Should I file the application first? Or take a test on U.S. history before I file the application?

Showing your knowledge of U.S. history is the fourth step. You need to file the application first.

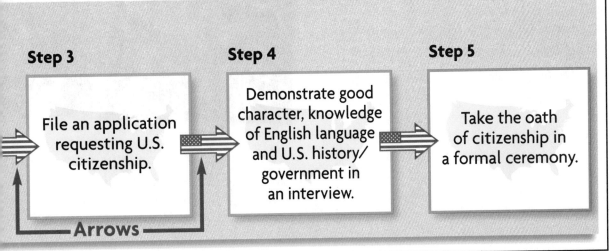

Step 3

File an application requesting U.S. citizenship.

Step 4

Demonstrate good character, knowledge of English language and U.S. history/ government in an interview.

Step 5

Take the oath of citizenship in a formal ceremony.

— Arrows —

The last step to becoming a new citizen of the United States is taking the oath of allegiance. This oath promises loyalty to the laws and Constitution of the United States of America. At this ceremony, new citizens also get a certificate that officially declares that they are citizens of the United States.

To become a citizen, an immigrant must have good moral character. Immigrants under 50 years of age must also be able to read, write, and speak English. Someone who wants to become a citizen must support the U.S. form of government and know about U.S. history and government.

Only U.S. citizens can vote in U.S. elections. Voters must be at least 18 years old.

The last step to becoming a new citizen of the United States

Read a Flowchart

Read the flowchart on pages 194–195 to answer these questions.

1. What is the first step in becoming a U.S. citizen?

2. What is the final step?

3. At which step in the process would a person be asked questions about the U.S. government?

4. During which step would a person take the oath of allegiance?

5. How many steps are in the process shown on pages 194–195?

6. Could an immigrant have an interview with INS if he or she has not lived in the United States for the required number of years?

7. At which step in the process is the application filed?

8. If an immigrant completed steps 1–4 but skipped step 5, would he or she be a citizen of the United States?

TEST TIP

If a test asks you to read a flowchart, be sure to read the steps in the right order. Carefully follow arrows and/or lines on the flowchart to make sure you understand the order of events.

HOW TO

Make a Graphic Organizer

Who's in Charge?

Have you ever wondered who makes the laws in this country? Who enforces those laws? Who makes decisions for your community, the national government or your state's government? Which systems and departments are managed by the individual states? Which ones are handled by the national government in Washington, D.C.?

In the United States, government power is divided between the federal (national) government and the states. The U.S. Constitution gives certain powers to the federal government. It reserves others for the states. For example, only the federal government can maintain an army and navy for the national defense.

On the other hand, only the state governments can make laws for marriage and divorce. State and federal governments share some powers, such as the building and repairing of public highways.

The division of powers can seem complicated. Using graphic organizers can help present information clearly. **Graphic organizers** are lines and shapes used to help organize facts and ideas. Concept maps, charts, graphs, spider maps, network trees, and events chains are some of the many types of graphic organizers.

Graphic organizers can be used to show data in school reports and presentations, or to organize information when studying for a test.

Use the following steps to make your own graphic organizer.

A **network tree** is a good way to show the relationship of facts or ideas to one another. The network tree below shows that the Constitution gives some powers to the federal government and reserves others for the states.

1 Decide What Information to Show

A graphic organizer does not tell everything you know about a subject. Instead, it organizes some facts or ideas to show their relationships to each other. Write down your topic and list the main ideas you want to include. Give your graphic organizer a title that tells the reader what it is about.

2 Choose a Type of Graphic Organizer

Decide which type of graphic organizer will work best to show the information. You might use a concept map, network tree, or Venn diagram.

3 Draw and Write

Draw the outline of your graphic organizer. Graphic organizers need words as well as lines, circles, and boxes. Put the topic and main ideas from your list into your graphic organizer in an order that makes sense. You may wish to start with main ideas and then add more specific details. The way information is organized will depend on the type of graphic organizer you use.

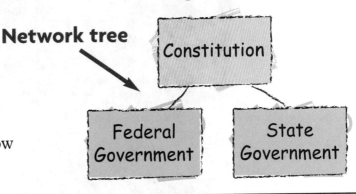

Dividing the Powers

Network tree

Constitution

Federal Government

State Government

EXAMPLE OF Making a Graphic Organizer

See how one student made a network tree listing state and federal powers.

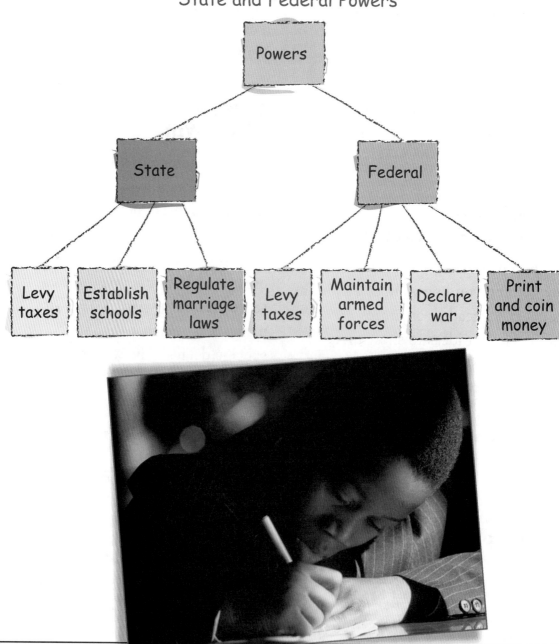

State and Federal Powers

Powers

State

Federal

Levy taxes

Establish schools

Regulate marriage laws

Levy taxes

Maintain armed forces

Declare war

Print and coin money

USE THIS SKILL

Make a Graphic Organizer

Use the information shown below to create a network tree or other kind of graphic organizer.

State and Federal Powers

State governments have the power to . . .

- Open new schools

- Make laws for marriage

- Make laws for divorce

- Make and enforce laws

- Collect employment taxes

- Maintain roads

The federal government has the power to . . .

- Tax imported goods

- Print money

- Maintain the military

- Declare war

- Make and enforce laws

- Collect employment taxes

- Maintain roads

TEST TIP   On a test you may be asked to make a graphic organizer. Think carefully about what type of organizer to use, and what information you should include.

Test-Taking
Strategies

Test-Taking Strategy
SKIMMING A PASSAGE

A mistake that many students make when taking tests is taking too long to read a passage. A **passage** is a short part of a writing, such as a paragraph or a very short story. On a test, you should **skim the passage.** This means you should read it quickly without trying to remember all the information. You can always look back at the passage when you have to answer questions. When you skim a passage, all you want to do is get an idea of what it is about. This is different from the kind of reading you do for fun or when studying.

Skim the paragraph below.

In June of 1776, Richard Henry Lee asked the colonies to come together and declare themselves free of Great Britain. John Adams supported this idea, and a committee of five was put together to write a resolution. Thomas Jefferson was the head of the committee. Its other members were John Adams, Benjamin Franklin, Robert R. Livingston, and Roger Sherman. Jefferson wrote a draft of a document on a portable writing desk he had designed himself. The draft was presented to the members of the First Continental Congress, who suggested some changes. After much arguing, the resolution was adopted on July 2. The formal Declaration of Independence was adopted on July 4, 1776.

What is the paragraph on page 204 mostly about? The answer is easy. The paragraph is mostly about the Declaration of Independence. Even though you just skimmed the paragraph, you could tell what it was about.

Who else besides Thomas Jefferson was on the committee to write the resolution? This is much harder because these names are details. You wouldn't remember them if you just skimmed the passage. Even if you tried to remember the names, you might still forget some of them. To answer the question, just look back at the paragraph. The other people on the committee were John Adams, Benjamin Franklin, Robert R. Livingston, and Roger Sherman.

How to skim a passage:

- Try to understand what the passage is mostly about.

- Don't worry about remembering details. You can go back and check the passage to answer questions.

- Try to figure out if the passage has a beginning, middle, and end. This will help you answer the questions later.

- If you come upon a word you don't understand, use the rest of the passage to guess its meaning. Don't waste time trying to figure it out.

- If a map, graph, or chart is part of the passage, just skim that, too. Try to understand how it fits with the rest of the passage. Don't try to memorize it. When you have to answer a question, look back at the map, graph, or chart.

Test-Taking Strategy
UNDERSTANDING SEQUENCE

Sequence means the order in which things happen. When you take a social studies test or even a reading test, many of the questions will be about sequence. Answers to sequence questions can almost always be found in the reading passage or on a time line that goes along with the passage.

Read the paragraph below.

Many important events are linked together. A good example is something that happened in 1908. Henry Ford began selling a car called the Model T for $850. This was much cheaper than other cars, so more people could afford one. Because so many people now had cars, it became necessary to improve roads. In addition, people started selling gasoline at service stations along the roads. Of course, none of this would have happened if Étienne Lenoir had not invented the first practical internal-combustion engine in 1860, long before the Model T.

Answer the question.

1. According to the paragraph, which of these came first?

   A. Improved roads

   B. The creation of the Model T

   C. The invention of the internal-combustion engine

   D. Selling gasoline at service stations along the roads

How to find the answer:

The first thing you have to do is read the question carefully. Remember, you are looking for the event that came first. Then you have to compare each answer choice to the paragraph.

- Answer **A** isn't right. The paragraph says that improved roads followed people having more cars, in this case, more Model T cars.

- Answer **B** might be right. The Model T is mentioned at the beginning of the paragraph, and you know it comes before answer **A.**

- Answer **C** is probably right. Even though it is mentioned at the end of the paragraph, the invention of the internal-combustion engine (1860) came **before** the Model T (1908).

- You know answer **D** is wrong. Service stations came last. They likely came after improved roads and more cars.

Now, there's one more thing to do. You must decide which choice is the right answer. Answer **B** might be right, and answer **C** is probably right. The dates you found in the paragraph tell you that answer **C** is the right answer.

STRATEGY TIP The sequence described in a passage may not always start at the beginning of the passage. Sometimes it jumps around, just like the passage about the Model T. Look for keywords like **before, after, while, same time, much later,** and **earlier.**

Test-Taking Strategy
MAKING COMPARISONS

Making comparisons is something you do every day. A simple comparison is this: Susan is taller than Brent. A comparison always involves at least two things. Some test questions ask you to compare two things that you read in a passage. Other test questions may ask you to compare information from graphs, charts, or maps.

Read the paragraph below.

When the European explorers first came to America, the Native Americans who lived here didn't understand how people could "own" land. In fact, they had a very different idea of "ownership" of everything. To the Native Americans, the land, the plants, and the animals were things to be used only as they were needed and they didn't belong to anyone. Europeans believed strongly in ownership, an idea that had a long tradition on other continents. In Europe, people had been fighting over the ownership of land for centuries. In America, there was plenty of land on which to live. If a drought came or the buffalo moved, the Native Americans just moved to a place that had more water or buffalo.

Answer the question.

1. Which comparison is made in the paragraph?

   A. How two cultures differed in their ideas of ownership

   B. Why Europeans lived longer than Native Americans

   C. What happened when Europeans came to America

   D. Why Native Americans moved more than Europeans

How to find the answer:

The question asks about a comparison. Remember, a comparison is about two things. This idea will help you find the right answer.

- Answer **A** compares two ideas about ownership. These ideas appear in the paragraph. This means answer **A** is probably right. You have to look at the other answer choices, however, just to make sure.

- Answer **B** is a comparison, but it isn't mentioned in the paragraph. In addition, you have no idea if it is right or wrong. Answer **B** can't be right.

- Answer **C** is about one thing Europeans found when they came to America. However, it isn't a comparison, so answer **C** is wrong.

- Answer **D** is tricky. It mentions two groups of people, Native Americans and Europeans, and it's a kind of comparison. However, this information is not explained in the paragraph. That means answer **D** isn't right.

After carefully reading all the answer choices, you will know that answer **A** is the right answer.

Test-Taking Strategy
SKIPPING DIFFICULT QUESTIONS

Not all the items on a test are equally difficult. Some are easier than others. It is important that you answer as many questions as you can. The best way to do this is to skip questions that are difficult and come back to them later. By doing this, you will be more likely to try all the questions. Remember, some of the questions at the end of a test might be easy, so it is important to try them before you run out of time.

Read the questions below.

Decide which one is easy and which one is difficult.

1. In the year A.D. 1, the world population was about 200 million. It just about doubled by A.D. 1000. By 1900, the population was estimated at more than one billion, but then jumped to two billion by 1930 and has continued to grow at a faster rate ever since. Which statement best describes the way the world population has changed since the year A.D. 1?

2. It is believed that the first people to reach the Americas arrived more than 10,000 years ago. They crossed a land bridge between Siberia and Alaska. This land bridge appeared during a period of cold called the Ice Age. So much water was frozen in glaciers and the polar ice caps that sea levels were lower than they are today. Which of these best compares the climate today and 10,000 years ago?

How to decide which question is more difficult:

Long questions are usually harder than short questions. However, both questions you looked at are about the same length. Things other than just length make one more difficult than the other.

- Number **1** contains a lot of numbers. They are confusing because they are dates and numbers, and the numbers are very large. It's hard to get a picture in your mind of the information in the question.

- Number **2** has only one number. It talks mostly about things you can understand easily, like geography and climate. It's easy to create a picture in your mind of mountains of ice and snow, a narrow piece of land, and people walking across the land bridge.

- The actual question for number **1** gives you little information. You will have to read all the answer choices. Because there is so much information in number **1,** the answer choices will probably be long and confusing. This will make number **1** even harder to answer.

- The question for number **2** asks you to think about something you already know, the climate today. It asks you to compare today's climate with the climate 10,000 years ago. You know it was colder then because this information is given. So, all you have to do is find the answer choice that says it was colder 10,000 years ago than it is now.

Number **2** is a much easier question. You should try to answer number **2** before you spend time trying to answer number **1.**

Test-Taking Strategy
USING KEYWORDS

Questions on tests often contain keywords. Answer choices on tests may also contain keywords. **Keywords** are important words that will help you find the right answer. Keywords are usually easy to find. They either tell you what you are supposed to be looking for or tell you where this information can be found.

Read the questions below. Find the keywords in each one.

1. What happened before the storm came?

2. In which year was Liberia established?

3. Which has a larger area, Canada or China?

4. What is Sequoya known for?

How to find the keywords:

1. The keyword is **before.** You know that the correct answer is something that took place **before** the storm, not after or during.

2. The two keywords are **Liberia established.** They tell you to look for information about Liberia, not another country. You should also look for when it was established, not when another event took place.

3. The keywords are **larger area.** Don't get confused and choose the one that is smaller or think about other information, like population.

4. The keyword is **Sequoya.** You should think about what he did, not what other people did.

Read the paragraph and use keywords to answer the questions.

Hundreds of years ago most roads in America were made of dirt or stone. When it rained, they became so muddy that horses and wagons couldn't use them. In some places, this problem was solved with plank roads. These were roads that were paved with pieces of wood! Logs or boards were laid down close together. They formed a surface that was bumpy, but at least people could ride on it during wet weather.

1. Which is true of plank roads?

   A. They were dusty.   B. They were bumpy.   C. They were made of brick.

How to find the keywords:

Read each of the answer choices. Look back at the paragraph above and find the sentences describing plank roads. Finding the keyword **bumpy** will help you choose **B** as the answer.

2. What problem did plank roads solve?

   A. Expensive travel   B. Getting lost   C. Muddy roads

How to find the keywords:

Read each of the answer choices. Read the paragraph again, checking to see if keywords in the answer choices are mentioned. As you read about the problem of **muddy** roads, you can easily select answer **C**.

Test-Taking Strategy
USING CONTEXT

When you read, there are times when you will come upon a word or phrase that you don't know. This can happen on a test, in a book, or with anything else you read. You can often use the meaning of the sentence or paragraph to help you understand the word or phrase. This is called **using context.**

Read the paragraph below.

> *The Louisiana Purchase was one of the most important events in American history. In 1803, the United States bought an enormous piece of land from France. President Thomas Jefferson sent Robert Livingston and James Monroe to France to negotiate the sale. Although they started out trying to buy just a small trading port, they eventually bought a huge area that doubled the size of the United States. The price of the purchase was $15 million, and it added 828,000 square miles of land to the United States, stretching from Louisiana to Montana.*

Answer the question.

1. The Louisiana Purchase involved an enormous piece of land. An *enormous* piece of land is:

   A. Small   B. Expensive   C. Dry   D. Large

How to find the answer:

Even if you don't know what *enormous* means, you can figure it out from the passage.

- Answer **A,** *small,* might be right, although it doesn't make sense with the rest of the paragraph. It's probably wrong, but let's look at the other answers.

- From the paragraph, you have no idea if *enormous* means "expensive." The price of the land was $15 million, but it was a lot of land. Answer **B** might be right, but another one might be better. Don't choose this answer yet.

- Answer **C,** *dry,* is probably not right. There is no information in the passage that tells you about the kind of land that was bought. This answer is probably wrong.

- Answer **D** is *large.* The paragraph says that Livingston and Monroe "bought a huge area." You probably know that huge means large. Also, the Louisiana Purchase doubled the size of the United States, suggesting that enormous means large. The correct answer is **D.**

 STRATEGY TIP The people who make tests almost always give you enough information to answer a question correctly. Always use the information provided to answer questions.

Test-Taking Strategy
WORKING CAREFULLY

It's easy to get nervous when you take a test. When you get nervous, you sometimes don't work as carefully as you should. Even if you know the right answer, you might make a mistake. That's why it is so important to work carefully.

STRATEGY TIP Feeling a little bit nervous when taking a test is good. It helps you get ready to do your best. If you have studied hard and work carefully, you will do well on a test.

Read the paragraph below.

The Great Depression was one of the most difficult times in American history. It occurred from 1929 to 1941 and began with a stock market collapse in 1929. Businesses stopped producing goods because they thought no one would buy them. They started firing workers, and soon no one could afford to buy things. People began to take all their money out of banks, and then the banks began to fail. What made the Great Depression even worse was a drought that hit the central part of the United States. It caused crops to fail so there was less food, and then the people who worked on farms didn't have work either.

Answer the question.

1. Which of these is not answered in the paragraph?

   A. How the Great Depression started

   B. How the Great Depression ended

   C. How long the Great Depression lasted

   D. What happened to workers in the Great Depression

How to find the answer:

Begin by looking at the question and the answer choices carefully. The question can be a little confusing because the word **not** is in the question. In other words, you are supposed to find the answer that is **not** mentioned in the paragraph.

- The paragraph says the Great Depression started in 1929. Answer **A** can't be right.

- Nothing in the paragraph talks about the end of the Great Depression. Answer **B** might be right, but you still have to look at the others.

- The paragraph says the Great Depression lasted from 1929 to 1941. Answer **C** isn't correct.

- Answer **D** can't be correct either because the paragraph talks about how workers were fired and didn't have work.

The correct answer is **B** because the paragraph doesn't talk about how the Great Depression ended. When you work carefully, it's easy to find the answer.

Test-Taking Strategy
TAKING THE BEST GUESS

Guessing is something we do every day. When you look outside and see that it is cloudy, you might guess that it is going to rain. When the phone rings and you are expecting a call from a friend, you guess who it is before answering the phone. When you take a test, you may also find it useful to guess. You should not guess the answer to every question, but if you aren't sure which answer is correct, you should guess rather than not answer.

STRATEGY TIP There are two times when you should guess on a test. The first time is when you are not sure which answer is correct. The second time is when the question asks you to take a guess by estimating or using given information.

Look at this graph. Use the graph to answer the questions on the next page.

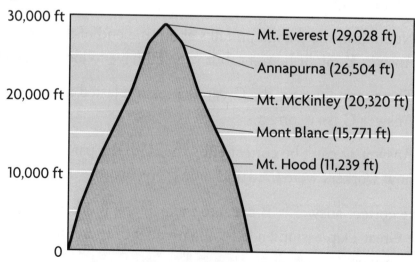

- Mt. Everest (29,028 ft)
- Annapurna (26,504 ft)
- Mt. McKinley (20,320 ft)
- Mont Blanc (15,771 ft)
- Mt. Hood (11,239 ft)

30,000 ft
20,000 ft
10,000 ft
0

Answer the question.

1. Pikes Peak is much taller than Mount Hood and only slightly shorter than Mont Blanc. Which of these is the best estimate of the height of Pikes Peak?

A. 14,110 ft

C. 12,057 ft

B. 16,823 ft

D. 11,194 ft

How to find the answer:

In this question, you are given enough information to find the answer, but you still must take a guess. An estimate is a guess that is based on information in a passage or on a graph. Sometimes an estimate is based on things you already know.

- Answer **A** looks pretty good. It is much taller than Mount Hood and a little bit shorter than Mont Blanc. This answer is a good estimate, but another answer might be better, so you have to look at all of the choices.

- You know at once that answer **B** is wrong. It is taller than Mont Blanc, so this answer can't be right.

- Answer **C** might be right. It is taller than Mount Hood and shorter than Mont Blanc. It is not as good as answer **A**, however, because it is closer to the height of Mount Hood and far from the height of Mont Blanc. So far, answer **A** is the best choice.

- You know at once that answer **D** is wrong. It is shorter than Mount Hood. The correct answer must be taller than Mount Hood.

Answer **A** is correct. You were able to guess or estimate this because of the information in the question and on the graph.

GLOSSARY

A

advertisement a method of giving information about a product or service, often used to encourage people to buy or use the product or service

B

bar graph a graphic tool using numbers, lines, and bars to compare two or more pieces of information

barter to trade or exchange goods or services without using money

biographical dictionary a reference source that gives facts about famous people, listing them alphabetically by last name

biography the story of a person's life

body the largest part of a news story, the body gives detailed information about the story. Also called *copy*.

boundary imaginary line that shows how land is divided into cities, states, countries, or territories

business letter a letter with a serious purpose

byline gives the name of the person who wrote a news story

C

capital the city where a state's government is located

cardinal directions the four main directions: North, South, East, and West

cause something that makes another thing happen

chart a graphic tool used to show information in an organized way

circle graph a graphic tool shaped like a circle and divided into sections. Circle graphs are used to show how an item or amount can be divided into parts.

citizen a native or legal resident of a country who has the rights and responsibilities provided by the laws of that country

city map a map that shows the important features of a city

civil rights the rights that all U.S. citizens have, as written in the U.S. Constitution

civil rights movement action taken by Americans who wanted African Americans to receive equal opportunities and fair treatment

classify a way to group objects, people, events, actions, or ideas based on something they have in common

climate the average weather conditions of a region over a period of time

climate map a map that uses pictures to give information about an area's weather patterns

closing sentence a sentence at the end of a paragraph that completes the main idea

comparing thinking about how people, things, events, or ideas are similar

comparison describes ways that two or more topics are the same

compass rose a symbol that shows direction on a map

conclusion a decision made based on evidence

Congress the lawmaking branch of the U.S. government, made of the Senate and the House of Representatives

continents the largest areas of land on Earth, usually large, unbroken masses of land

contrast to describe ways that two or more topics are different

contrasting thinking about how people, events, or ideas are different

copy the largest part of a news story, the copy gives detailed information about the story. Also called *body.*

country a political term meaning a nation or independent territory

cultural map a map that shows the place or places where different social groups live or have lived

culture the way of life, customs, arts, beliefs, and languages shared by a group of people

D

decision a choice made by making a judgment or coming to a conclusion

demand the amount of an item that people are willing and able to buy at different prices

description a way to make a picture with words and tell about a writer's thoughts, feelings, or experiences

desert a dry area on Earth where few plants and animals live

diagram a graphic tool used to show and explain information

division of labor a large task or job is divided into many smaller tasks or jobs so that more work can be done in a shorter amount of time

dry a climate region having very little rainfall or snowfall

E

economy the way money, products, and services are made and used by people in a certain area

edit correcting errors in spelling, grammar, and punctuation

effect something that happens as a result of a cause

encyclopedia a reference source that gives general information about important people, topics, places, and events

ending the last part of a news story, the ending tells the outcome of an event, how a problem was solved, or what could happen next

endorsement the use of a famous person to help sell a product or service

evidence facts that give information about an event

F

fact a true statement that can be checked or proven

flowchart a graphic tool that shows the steps of a process in order

G

gathering grid a simple chart used to sort information

geometric boundary boundary made by people, such as a political border between countries

graphic organizer lines and shapes used to help organize facts and ideas

grid identifier the letter and number combination used to identify a place on a grid

grid map a map that uses sets of crisscrossing lines to divide the map into squares, then uses letters and numbers to identify the squares

H

headline the title of a news story, it tells a reader what the story is about

high latitude a climate region where summers are very short

highland a climate region at a high elevation with many mountains

historical fiction a realistic story set in the past, often written about real people and events in history

historical map a map that shows the features, boundaries, or events of a region's past

I

immigrants people who come to a new country to live

intermediate directions the directions in between each of the four main directions, intermediate directions are: Northeast, Northwest, Southeast, and Southwest

Internet a worldwide computer network

Internet Service Provider (ISP) a company that connects a person's computer to the Internet

island area of land surrounded by water

J

journal a place for a person to write about daily events in his or her life

journal entry a section of writing from a journal, usually covering one day or other period of time

K

key tells what the symbols on a map represent. Also called a *legend.*

keywords important words that give information about questions, answers, or both; words related to a subject or topic

L

label a word or words naming different parts of a diagram or passage

landform a natural feature on the surface of Earth

lead the first paragraph in a news story, where important facts are given

legend tells what the symbols on a map represent. Also called a *key.*

line diagram a graphic tool that uses lines, words, and symbols to show relationships between concepts or ideas

line graph a graphic tool that uses dots connected by a line to show how something changes over time

loaded words words that are used to persuade without giving facts

M

making comparisons comparing two or more things to one another to find similarities or differences

map scale a bar or line that shows how to measure distances on a map

midlatitude a climate region having warm summers and colder winters

mountain high, sloping, often rocky landform

N

natural boundary boundary made by bodies of water and/or landforms, such as oceans, rivers, or mountain ranges

network tree a graphic tool used to show the relationship of facts and ideas to one another

New England a region of the northeastern United States, including the states of Maine, New Hampshire, Vermont, Massachusetts, Rhode Island, and Connecticut

news story a report on a current event

O

opinion a statement of what someone believes or feels

oral report a spoken presentation about a single topic, delivered in person to a live audience

outline a written plan used to organize notes and ideas into main topics and detailed subtopics

P

paragraph a group of two or more sentences that tells about one main idea

passage a short part of a writing, such as a paragraph or short story

physical map a map that shows the natural features of a place, such as landforms and bodies of water

picture diagram a graphic tool that uses pictures to show how things work or how they are related to one another

plain large, flat area of land

point of view a personal way of looking at the world, including a person's own thoughts, feelings, and opinions

political map a map that shows the boundaries that people have created, such as border lines around countries, states, or cities

product map a map that shows the goods that are made or grown in a certain area

Q

quantity demanded the amount of a product or service that people want to buy at any one time

quantity supplied the amount of a product or service that is for sale at any one time

quote the exact words that someone has said

R

reference source a book or other source that gives facts about many different subjects

regional map a map that shows an entire area where the land or culture has common features

report a presentation, spoken or in writing, about a single topic

representative a member of the House of Representatives in the U.S. Congress

revise to make changes to the content of a written passage, such as adding or deleting information

road map a map that shows the streets, highways, and points of interest in a city, state, province, or country

S

scenic highway a roadway that allows travelers to see the natural beauty of areas around the roadway

search engine program that helps people do word searches on the World Wide Web

segregation a system of setting people apart from one another because of race

senator a member of the lawmaking branch of U.S. government, the Senate in the U.S. Congress

sentence outline a written plan used to organize notes and ideas, using complete sentences

sequence the order in which things happen

skim the passage to read a passage quickly to get an idea of what it is about

state map a map showing the important features of a state

subject the person about whom a story is written

subject headings headings that explain what a passage is about

subtopics information that is included about a main topic in a written passage or on an outline

summary a collection of main ideas about a topic

T

taking notes writing down important facts, ideas, and opinions about a topic while reading, listening, watching, or thinking

thematic map a map that focuses on one main theme, or subject

time line a type of diagram that lists dates and events along a line in the order that they took place

time periods portions of time, such as a number of years, weeks, days, or hours

time sequence the order in which events take place

title a word or phrase that tells what a diagram shows, tells what a map is showing, or tells what a written passage is about

topic sentence a sentence that introduces the main idea of a paragraph

tropical a climate region having warm temperatures and a large amount of rainfall

U

using context using the general meaning of a sentence or paragraph to help you understand the meaning of a word or phrase

V

valley low area of land, often near mountains and hills

Venn diagram a graphic tool that uses two overlapping circles to compare and contrast information

volumes individual books, tapes, or discs that make up a set

volunteers people who give their time and skills to help others

W

work in a group work with other people to achieve a common goal

World Wide Web (www) a part of the Internet that allows people to easily connect to various Web sites. Usually seen abbreviated as www.

X
Y
Z

INDEX

Credits